England's Festivals

A Year of Seasons, Customs and Traditions

B. E. Mayne

(aka Brian Everett Mayne)

i

Acknowledgements

I wish to acknowledge a very large debt to the many earlier writers on the subjects of the seasons, calendar customs, saints' days and agricultural and pastoral activities. Notable among these are Miss Christina Hole, for her dedicated researches and many publications in the field of folk studies, Mr. Laurence Whistler (*The English Festivals*), for breathing life into the major dates involved and Chambers' *Book of Days* for an overall structure and history to the year from a mid-19th century perspective. For an acquaintance with many of the earlier writers, thanks go to the resources of the British Library and to the very fine collection at the library of the Folklore Society.

I am also grateful to the Youth Hostels Association (England and Wales), whose facilities allowed me to see many of the locations and natural seasonal settings described herein.

Extracts taken from the *King James Version of the Bible*, which is Crown Copyright, are reproduced with permission.

Illustrations for the cover (Morris Dance) and through the months are from *The Book of Days,* Chambers, Robert (ed.), 1863-4, with the exception of
  - The first Christmas card is from one used by Wikipedia and
  - The map of traditional English Counties is from http://commons.wikimedia.org/wiki/File:English_geographical_counties_1889_(named).svg. This file is licensed under the Creative Commons Attribution-Share Alike 3.0 Unported license. Attribution: Dr Greg.

This book was originally written in the early 1980s, and then reviewed and revised prior to publication of this edition to make it more permanently available to a wider audience. However, some entries may still inadvertently reflect practices and other observations which were current at the time of the original writing, rather than that of the date of publication. In addition to changes in some of the calendar customs, farming practices and the proliferation of imported fruit and vegetables have evolved dramatically since the early 1980s.

Despite all of the help from sources and individuals, the author accepts responsibility for errors and shortcomings, and would be grateful for any suggestions respecting possible corrections and improvements.

- B. E. M. (May 2012)
  (bemayne@gmail.com)

Table of Contents

SELECT CALENDAR OF CUSTOMS AND FESTIVALS
(Note: Moveable ones are placed in their approximate calendar settings)

<u>Custom/Feast Day</u>	<u>Date</u>	<u>Location</u>
<u>January</u>		
First Foot	1st	The North
Cream of the Well	1st	
Burning of the Bush	1st	Herefordshire, Worcestershire
Presenting mistletoe to the cow first calving	1st	
Twelfth Night/Epiphany	5th	
- Twelfth Night Fires		West Midlands
- Wassailing Oxen		Herefordshire, Worcestershire
- Twelfth Cake		
Ploughtide	Sunday next	
Plough Monday/St. Distaff	Monday next	
- Plough Matches		
- Sword Dances		The North
- Fool Plough Procession		
- Corn Dolly		
Wassailing Orchards	16th	Southwest
St. Vincent's Day	22nd	
St. Paul's Conversion	25th	

<u>**February**</u>

Celtic Imbolc	**1st**	
Candlemas Eve **- Candle-bearing/Feast of Lights**	**1st**	
Candlemas	**2nd**	
Cradle-Rocking	**2nd**	**Blidworth,**
Nottinghamshire		
Wives' Feast Day	**2nd**	**The North**
St. Blaise **- Blessing the Throat** **- Wool Town Processions**	**3rd**	
St. Valentine	**14th**	

Blessing the Salmon Net
  Fisheries
	14th	**Norham-on-Tweed,**
		          Northumberland

King's Lynn Mart	**14th**	**King's Lynn, Norfolk**
St. Matthias Planting	**24th**	
St. Oswald	**28th/29th**	**Worcestershire**

<u>**March**</u>

Lent	**Moveable**
Shrovetide	**Moveable**
Shrove Tuesday/Pancake Day	**Moveable**

- Cockfighting
- Thrashing the Hen
- Throwing at Cocks
- Lent Crocking   Notably the Southwest
- Shroving Processions
- Hurling   The North and Southwest
- Pancake Races   Olney, Buckinghamshire

Ash Wednesday   Moveable
- Jack-a-Lent
- Marble Season begins

St. David's Day   1st

St. Patrick's Day   17th

Medieval Mystery Play   17th

Lady Day   25th

Tichborne Dole   25th   Tichborne,
    Hampshire

Mothering Sunday   Moveable

<u>April</u>

All Fools' Day   1st

Palm Sunday   Moveable

Passion Week   Moveable
- Maundy Thursday   Moveable
- Good Friday   Moveable
    - Hot Cross Buns
    - Marble Day   Tinsley Green, West Sussex
    - Long Rope Day   Southeast

- Easter   Moveable
       - Easter Eggs
       - Egg-Shackling   Yorkshire, Lancashire, The
North
       - Egg-Rolling   Yorkshire,
Lancashire, The North
       - Pace-Egging   The North
       - Easter Egg Hunt
       - Hare Pie Scrambling
       - Hare Hunts
       - Easter Lifting

Hocktide   Moveable

Hearing the First Cuckoo   About 21st

St. George's Day   23rd

St. Mark's Day   25th

<u>May</u>

May Day   1st
- Celtic Beltane   West, Southwest, Isle of
Man
- Ramroasting legend   Holne, Devonshire
- Roman Floralia Remnants   King's Lynn, Norfolk;
                                           Horncastle, Lincolnshire
- Maying
- May Garlands   1st
                                   (Old Style) Abbotsbury, Dorset
- May Queen   1st   Various, notably
Bedfordshire
- Parading the Jack
- Lord and Lady of the May   Midlands
- May Lady
- Maypole
- Morris Dancers
- Mumming Plays   Padstow, Cornwall and

- Robin Hood   Minehead, Somerset

- Hobby Horses

- Chimney-Sweep's Holiday   Notably London
- Helston Furry Dance   Saturday   Helston,
                             Nearest 8th Cornwall
- Battle of Winter and May 1st   Isle of Man
- May Day Hymns   Southampton and
        Oxford

St. Dunstan/Frankan   19th

St. Urban   25th

Rogationtide   Moveable
 - Beating the Bounds

Ascension Day   Moveable
 - Well-Dressing   Derbyshire (notably
                             Tissington) and the West
Oak Apple Day   29th

June

Whitsuntide   Moveable
 - Whitsun Ales/Church Ales
 - Whitsun Mystery Plays   (Whitweek)   Notably
        Chester
 - Dunmow Flitch   (Whit Monday) Great Dunmow,
Essex
 - Ram Roasting Fair   (Whit Monday)
        Kingsteinton, Devonshire
 - Bread and Cheese
        Distribution   (Whit Sunday) St. Briavels,
        Gloucestershire
 - Cheese Rolling   Spring Bank   Brockworth,
                             Holiday   Gloucestershire

Trinity Sunday Moveable
 - **Lamb Ales** Trinity Monday Kirtlington,
  Oxfordshire

Corpus Christi Day Moveable

St. Barnabas's Day 11th

**Midsummer's Day/Birth
  of St. John the Baptist** 24th
 - **Midsummer's Eve Bonfires
    and Torch Parades** 23rd Cornwall
 - **Well-Dressing** Thursday
     near 24th Buxton, Derbyshire
 - **Tap-Dressing** Saturday
     near 24th Youlgrave, Derbyshire

 - **St. John's Eve** 23rd
 - **Druid Service** Solstice Dawn Stonehenge

St. Peter's Day 29th
 - **Rush-strewing** 28th Barrowden,
   Leicestershire
 - **Rush-bearing** 29th Warcop, Cumbria
 - **Hay-strewing** Sunday
     after 29th Wingrave,
  Buckinghamshire

<u>**July**</u>

**Midsummer's Fires
 (Midsummer's Eve, Old Style)** 4th Walton,
  Northumberland

Bawming the Thorn 5th Appleton
  Thorn, Chesire

Proclaiming Prior Year's Laws 5th Tynwald Hall,
  Isle of Man

Hay Strewing | Thursday after 5th | Leicestershire

Lot Meadow Mowing | Early July | Yarnton, Oxfordshire

Hay Strewing | Sunday near 15th | Old Weston Church, Cambridgeshire

Rushbearing | Last Saturday Of July | Ambleside, Cumbria

Fairlop Oak Festival | First Friday Of July | Hainault Forest, Essex

St. Swithin's Day | 15th

Horn Fair | 25th | Ebernoe, Sussex

St. James's Day | 25th

Oyster-Shell Day | 25th

Cherry Fairs | End of July

Lammas Fairs | Tuesday before 3rd Thursday | Exeter, Devonshire

August

Peter's Pence | 1st

Lammas Day | 1st
- Celtic Lugnasad
- Lammastide Sheep Fairs
- Lammas Services | 1st Sunday

St. Oswald (of Northumbria)   5th
 - **Clipping the Church**   **Guiseley,**
     Yorkshire
 - **Rush Strewing**   **Saturday**
           near 5th   **Grasmere, Cumbria**

Grand Wardmote   **Early August**   **Meriden,**
    Warwickshire

St. Bartholomew's Day   24th
 - **Bartholomew Fairs** **Near 24th**   **Smithfield, London**
                    and others
 - **Burning the Bartle**   **Saturday**
           near 24th   **West Witton, Yorkshire**

Plague Memorial Service   **Last Sunday**   **Eyam,**
    Derbyshire

September

St Giles' Fair   **Following 1st**
          Sunday
          after 1st   **Oxford**

Start of Oyster Season   1st   **Colchester, Essex**

Horn Dance   **Following 1st**
          Sunday
          after 4th   **Abbots Bromley,**
                  Staffordshire

Nutting on Holy Rood Day   14th

Clipping the Church   **Sunday**   **Near 19th**   **Painswick,**
    Gloucestershire

St. Matthew's Day   21st

Harvest   **After corn harvest**
- Crying the Mare
- Corn Dolly
- Hock Cart and Harvest Queen

- Harvest Home
- Harvest Thanksgiving Service   Late September/
                                 early October

Michaelmas Day   29th
- Michaelmas Goose
- Hiring Fairs
- Michaelmas Eve Nut-Cracking 28th

October

Bellringers' Feast   7th   Twyford, Hampshire

St. Luke's Day   18th

St. Crispin's and
     St. Crispinian's Day   25th

St. Jude's Day   28th

All Hallow's Eve   31st
- Hallowe'en Guisers and lantern-
     Bearing Processions   West Country,
        esp. Hinton St. George, Somerset
- Hallowe'en Games
- Hallowe'en Superstitions

November

Feast of All Saints   1st

Celtic Samhain   1st

All Soul's Day   2nd
 - Souling and Soul-caking

Guy Fawkes' Night   5th
- Swinging a Guy
- Rolling of the Tar Barrels   **Ottery St. Mary,**
          Devonshire
- Ringing Night   **Spelsbury, Oxfordshire**
- Searching the
      Houses of Parliament   **prior to annual opening   London**

 - Mischief Night   4th

Martinmas   11th
- Wroth Silver   **Knightlow Cross, Near**
                              Dunchurch, Warwickshire

- Pack-rag Day

St. Clement's Day   23rd

St. Catherine's Day   25th

St. Andrew's Day   30th

Advent and Advent Images **Sunday**
                         near 30th

<u>**December**</u>

St. Nicholas's Day   6th
- Boy Bishops

St. Lucy's Day   13th
- Last Ember Day

St. Thomas's Day   21st
- Thomassing

Geographic Map of Traditional English Counties (1889)

Source: Wikimedia - see acknowledgements for link and attribution

xx

Introduction

This book is a journey through England's year. It explores the seasons, the rhythm of rural activities and the evolution of the various calendar festivals which this island's inhabitants have associated with the year since before history began to be recorded.

It is a complex story. The customs described owe bits and pieces of their characters to each of the many different peoples who settled in England and to the cycle of the year itself. None of the rituals involved is fixed. Through the centuries each has undergone varying degrees of change. Some have been discontinued while others, seemingly more fashionable, have entered the roster. There are a few instances of customs having emigrated to distant corners of the Empire where they still survive, though they disappeared from our own scene centuries ago. In other cases they have returned home, but have been so altered by their exposure to another land and climate that they are hardly recognisable for what they were when they left us.

Most of the major festivals which we still celebrate today have, as their earliest sources, the ancient pastoral and agricultural calendars which dominated the primitive English countryside. The Celtic pastoral calendar had four major festivals: *Imbolc* (February 1) for lambing; *Beltane* (May 1) marking the first grazing of the year; *Lugnasad* (August 1) for the end of shearing; and *Samhain* (November 1) for the rounding up of flocks and the slaughtering of surplus sheep for which there was insufficient winter fodder. These celebrations have mostly been Christianised and are observed now as Candlemas on February 2, May Day, Lammastide and Martinmas.

The agricultural calendar gradually supplanted the pastoral one and divides the year into quarters, roughly coincident with the solstices and equinoxes. Its main festivals are remembered now as Lady Day (March 25), Midsummer's Day (June 24), Michaelmas (September 29), and Christmas (December 25).

The principle festivals have always been religious in nature. They were observed as an act of worship or as a means of giving thanks to an unknowable Intelligence. It is natural, then, that the major alterations that have been made to them have come about as results of religious change itself.

It is difficult to find a custom of note that was not pagan at one time and has not since been baptised by the Christian Church. Virtually all of them were celebrated by the Saxons, Normans, Romans, Danes and Celts long before any of those peoples had ever heard of Christianity. When Augustine made his first English converts in the sixth century, he had explicit instructions from Pope Gregory that the older customs not be eradicated, but rather redirected to Christian ends as a means of gradually weaning the heathen spirit toward the new religion. Much later, after the Reformation, the Puritans had no such qualms. They zealously and drastically uprooted any festival they considered an abuse, or even an enjoyment, of worship.

Through a laborious and sometimes torturous historical route, we are today heirs to a very intricate ecclesiastical calendar. It borrows from both solar and lunar revolutions in its annual round of fixed and moveable feasts. The fixed feasts are principally a means of honouring the growing roster of saints, while the two moveable cycles of Easter and Christmas remind us of the chronology of the essential New Testament events.

The history of the calendar itself is an intriguing one. Through an omission on the part of Julius Caesar's astronomer, Sosigenes, the Julian Calendar allowed an error to creep in which amounted to one day every four hundred years. By the time Pope Gregory XIII corrected this in 1582, a full ten days had to be adjusted for. He made this correction by the simple expediency of omitting ten days from the calendar that year.

However, non-Roman Catholic countries, like England, obstinately refused to accept the change on the grounds that it had been sanctioned by the Bishop of Rome. In 1752 an Act of Parliament finally recognised the Gregorian Calendar, but the delay had been such, one hundred and seventy years, that an elimination of eleven days was then required. Because of this legislation, an early part of September, 1752, does not exist in English history. Humbler folk greeted this news with the threats of riots. They interpreted the Act as meaning that eleven days of sunshine would be lost to the crops, that they would be robbed of eleven days wages and, incredibly, that they were all doomed to die eleven days earlier than necessary. Common cries to unpopular politicians at that time were: "Who stole the eleven days?" and "Give us back the eleven days!"

There is an interesting deduction to be drawn from the eighteenth century eleven-day adjustment. Any inherited weatherlore that predates it and is tied to the calendar is obviously going to be wrong. For example, the 40-day rain forecast to follow St. Swithin's, July 15, is based on a date that was already out some days from the real date when he died in the ninth century, and then became further out as time marched on; and then altered completely with the calendar change. Similarly, any villager who 'experienced' Halloween ghosts on a pre-1752 Eve of All Saints can be said to have had a fairly vivid imagination (or were experiencing *non*-Halloween ghosts).

In spite of the protests, the New Style calendar has long been accepted and we are today more open to scientific refinements which improve the measurement of time. This is fortunate, as adjustments to the year are still going on. Since 1972 there have been further adjustments for the 'leap seconds' that have brought the earth's slightly uneven rotation back in line with solar time.

Although the natural cycle of the year follows season upon season with a regularity that defies mankind's ability to observe it as accurately as we might wish to, the numerous folk customs which still survive continue to change and evolve as we go on in our attempt to fit current fashion and temperament to special dates in the annual round. The Christmas tree and card illustrate the point. Well under two hundred years ago they were virtually unknown in England. Now their absence is the exception rather than the rule.

Oddly enough, although the influence of the Empire had a tremendous impact in spreading many of these customs around the globe, its decline has not had a similar negative effect on their practice. Today's sun still never sets on the major English festivals. But the credit for this is probably mostly due to the fact that almost without exception each of these customs predated the Empire and was meant to harmonise with the natural annual cycle itself.

The evolution continues. Parliament has debated whether to change the date of the May Day Bank Holiday or to abolish it altogether. Meanwhile, some employers have been agitating to have some bank holidays chopped from the present list. From their points of view this makes sense. Around 1950, it was practice for employees to expect only two weeks annual leave, and those usually in August. Consequently, the six bank holidays formed important leisure points in balancing out the rest of the year. Now, annual leaves given are much more generous and begin again to approach the eight weeks enjoyed in the twelfth century by farm labourers who had never heard of a bank.

After all, what is a bank holiday? It was originally meant to be a day when banks and other financial institutions closed. Its precedent did not give employees of other industries the right to a day off. But the bank holiday came to be applied and expected so universally that it has gradually eclipsed the older round of religious feasts and fasts. Many of the Whitsuntide customs are presently observed on the Spring Bank Holiday, while Lammastide is virtually forgotten now with the later bank holiday given in August. We have developed a consciousness in which the major punctuation points to the year have become bank holidays and there is an obvious corollary in that we have learned to associate a laying down of tools with currency and commerce rather than with the solar and religious cycles. Like the changes in the celebrations which occurred with the advents of Augustine and the Puritans, an objective alien observer might well surmise that our religion has adopted itself in such a way that our 'holy days' now centre around what we consider another, more powerful, god.

Fortunately, the history of bank holidays is outside of the scope of this volume. Here, the subject matter concentrates on festivals which have deeper meanings and require the active emotional involvement and physical participation of all celebrants.

One day, when currency has been fully replaced by electronic blips, some future historian may endeavour to explain the sense and significance of 'bank holidays.' It will be an unenviable task. In terms of the metaphysical spirit which graces the seasonal religious festivities, a search for meaning in the bank holiday will have much the same point as a quest for the soul in an autopsy.

While the subject matter of this book is focussed on England, major relevant customs from the Isle of Man are included. With these geographic constraints, there was still an understandable difficulty in deciding where true boundaries really are in the matter of folk customs. Some extend to Wales, Scotland, Ireland, and even around the world to former colonies. Others which are practiced here have arisen from influences external to England. This is particularly true in the North, where there are close links to Scottish usages. But many more owe their origins to Rome and to all those lands in which today's English peoples have their roots. Another note concerning geography is that the bulk of references in this volume are to the traditional English counties, whose boundaries have been altered since World War II. New boundaries have been ignored as they have, as far as is known, yet had no relevant contribution to make in the evolution of such traditional festivals.

As the aim of this narrative has been to provide an overview of those practices which are linked to the rhythm of the natural year, this effort is not exhaustive in describing all customs, or even in the treatment of individual ones. The emphasis has been on annual celebrations that embrace all participants in their spirit, rather than on spectator events such as ceremonies of state or important annual sporting dates. Usually, where feasible, the first mention of a custom has been entered in **bold** to facilitate locating it, especially for those who wish to use the book for referencing individual customs.

The individual monthly chapter length is not necessarily a measure of its festive importance. The same holds true as respects the number of pages it has taken to describe any particular custom. Just because twice as many pages may have been written on Christmas and its preparations as were devoted to May Day, does not infer the latter is half as important as the former. The length of narrative allotted to each has been a result of a complex weighting of their individual histories, characters and the spirit in which they have been and are observed. Easter, for example, although being a major pivotal point in the ecclesiastical year, has taken only about one-quarter of the room occupied by the pagan May Day. And the celebration of Ascension Day, which one would think should be even more auspicious than that of Easter, has required only about half the space devoted to the Resurrection.

The sequence of months used follows our present calendar year: January to December. However, there may be some readers who are disposed to follow another cycle. For the farmer, the New Year begins after the harvest. The Celts and Saxons both began their years at different times. And, a little over two centuries ago, the English year did not legally begin until Lady Day on March 25. For these reasons, while there is continuity through the narrative, it has been written so that the reader may begin at any month desired and follow the year from there.

In spite of the gradual shift toward an urban-oriented English population, it is astonishing how many of the festivities described are still alive. Some of the survivals are relics, with the participants merely moving mechanically through the motions involved. But a very large number of them are extant today because the spirit that animates them continues to be transmitted live from one generation to the next.

Perhaps it is because of creeping urbanisation that we cling all the more to the meaning and stability which the English festivals lent our ancestral year. Our great-great grandfathers, though perhaps rustic and relatively 'uneducated,' inherited a good deal of wisdom, which had been handed down from one yeoman farmer to the next.

In the cities we are dispossessed, having no similar rural – or even urban - heritage of wisdom bequeathed to us. A renewed acquaintance with these older traditional celebrations will allow us to judge their respective values and, hopefully, lend a heightened sense of awareness and appreciation for the round of seasons everyone, rural and urban alike, travels through each year.

JANUARY

The blackest month of all the year
Is the month of Janiveer.

Our Saxon ancestors originally called this month *Wolf-monat*, or 'Wolf month' as, because of the cold and snow and the scarcity of other animals to feed upon, it was more likely in this month for people to be attacked and devoured by wolves than in any other month of the year. Later on, in a more civilised frame of mind, they renamed it *Aefter-Yule*, or 'After Christmas.' It is curious that, while their names for the months did not survive the Norman Conquest, we have retained a Saxon heritage in our days of the week, which they named for planetary bodies and for their pagan gods: Moon's Day, Tiw's Day, Woden's Day, Thor's Day, Friga's Day, Seater's Day and Sun's Day.

The name January was given by the second Roman King, Numa Pompilius, who reigned in the seventh century, B.C. and who added two new months to the calendar. This one was named in honour of Janus, the god of openings, whose two faced bust appeared over archways and doors, one face looking forward and the other backward. It was the same King Pompilius who decreed that January be the first month of the year. By the earlier Jewish, Greek and Egyptian calendars it would have been the eleventh month, for their new year began at the end of March, and January's position originally followed that of February. The Jewish March 25 still continued to be recognised as the first of the year legally in most Christian countries, including England although, popularly, the new year started in January. It wasn't until 1752 that the legal year in Britain started on January 1. Before that, one would date the days between January 1 and March 24 as, for example, February 14, 1723-4, meaning that legally it was 1723, but popularly 1724 had already started.

January follows close upon the heels of the winter solstice, its lengthening days proclaiming the start of a new cycle. In rural England, the month conjures up images of frost on the window panes, smoke curling above a thatched roof, a pint of beer by a crackling hearth, and visions of steaming mutton and boiled beef. The weather alternates between freezing and thawing and, as the days become longer, it is generally believed they also grow colder. Chambers, in the 1860s in his *Book of Days*, paints a dismal picture of January in England: "You pass the village churchyard and almost shiver to think that the very dead who lie there must be pierced by the cold, for there is not even a crimson hip or haw to give a look of warmth to the stark hedges, through which the bleak wind whistles." The frozen weather, though, is welcomed by the young at heart, as the ice and snow lend themselves to the age-old pleasures of snow-balling, sliding, tobogganing, skating and curling.

January has its lighter side, too, in the traditional customs and festivals through which our ancestors, from time immemorial, have broken its cheerless monotony. The hard toil involved in the old agricultural cycle naturally gave rise to its particular celebrations. The coming of the Christian Church changed the names of some and added others, usually in the form of feast days and Saints' days. Even more have been included to the roster more recently, commemorating events which have little to do with the older rural life.

The annual round of customs begins on January 1, almost as a tribute to the sly English humour, implying that resolutions solemnly made on New Year's Eve must quickly be broken before life's enjoyment is too far eroded. New Year's Day celebrations derive from the week long Roman Saturnalia that followed the winter solstice. Although frowned upon by the Church, Roman inspired bacchanalian festivities survived in some parts of England into the late Middle Ages.

Being January 1, this first day of the year's celebrations is superstitiously connected with prophecies concerning the year ahead.

In many parts of England, but more particularly in the North, the first visitor to enter a house traditionally has been reputed to have the power of influencing its fortunes for the next year. The ceremony is still kept up at some locations with a prearranged **First Foot** arriving at just after midnight bearing gifts that are symbolic of food, drink and fuel. The gifts are usually some bread and a piece of coal. Sometimes a coin is included to ensure prosperity. There are many superstitions attached to the First Foot, depending mostly on the region the custom is practiced in, but, generally, a dark-haired man is said to bring the best luck, so long as he is not empty-handed. If he is cross-eyed, fair or if the First Foot is a woman, ill fortune is supposed to follow. The worst First Foot has customarily been one whose eyebrows meet. Such individuals were thought to bring bad luck, and it was believed they would not live long enough to marry. A First Foot should normally be someone not living at the house, but when that cannot be arranged, a male member of the household will be let out just before the New Year has struck, and be re-admitted just after, bearing the gifts of good fortune.

The **Cream of the Well**, also known as the **Flower of the Well**, is another first of the year custom. In it, the first water drawn from a well, spring or the closest other water source in the New Year brings good fortune to he or she who draws it and, if bottled and kept in the house, acts as a charm for the whole family. If a young girl is first to 'Cream the Well,' a marriage is indicated for her before the year is out. A well or spring that serves several families offers some competition on who will be first to it after the New Year has struck. An especially hopeful Creamer will station him/herself by the well before midnight to be first when the New Year arrives. In Northumberland, after drawing the Cream of the Well, it is practice to throw a propitiatory offering of grass into the water, which serves as a sign to subsequent hopefuls that the Flower has already been drawn.

Another popular New Year's Day custom is called the **Burning of the Bush**. It has, unfortunately, almost disappeared in the last hundred years. At around five am a globe of hawthorn (in Hertfordshire), or a crown made of blackthorn (in Worcestershire), along with a sprig of mistletoe that had hung in the farmhouse kitchen since the previous New Year's Day, would be taken out and burnt in the first-sown wheat field. In addition to symbolising the Crown of Thorns, the Bush had the dual function of having protected the house from ill-fortune during the prior year and, through the ritual burning, purifies the soil and protects the crops for the coming year. In some regions the celebrants would gather around the fire crying "Auld Cider!" and toast it with cider and cakes provided by the farmer. Meanwhile, a new Bush would be made and have its ends scorched in the fire. It, along with a fresh branch of mistletoe, would be hung in its traditional place in the farmhouse kitchen.

The Druids considered the oak tree to be sacred, and the mistletoe which grew on it was so revered it was only to be ceremonially cut with a golden instrument. The mistletoe's pagan associations in both Norse mythology and the Celtic religion led to its being forbidden in most early churches. Such has its link with fertility been that, up until recently, it has been a tradition to take a sprig from the bunch of **mistletoe** kept in the house for the prior year and **present** it **to the cow first calving** after New Year' Day. This is thought to lead to a fruitful year for the whole herd. A new bunch of mistletoe replaces the old one after the Burning of the Bush.

Rural wildlife forms another facet of England's January. A careful observer can decipher tracks in the snow near their water sources of otters, foxes, badgers, deer, hedgehogs, grey squirrels, hares, rabbits, shrews, moorhens, herons, wild duck, pheasants, partridge, crows and other small birds. If the weather is bad enough, owls can be seen hunting by day, and the tracks of foxes move closer to the farmer's poultry houses and rubbish heaps. As there is no foliage on the trees, January is the best time to observe the smaller birds and the rich and colourful variety of English mosses. The smallest of British birds, the golden-crested wren and the wag-tail, stay with us all through the winter. The birds make their meals of haws and other fruit still clinging to trees and bushes. Holly berries are usually left to the last of the month, not as a dessert, but as an 'enforced Lent,' when the birds can find nothing better to eat. The songs of wrens, pewits and robins fill the air. Mistle thrushes can be heard from a great distance, while starlings are known for the variety of sounds they make as they whistle and chatter to their fellows. Rooks make their sallies in groups, going from their nests in the woods to their feeding grounds and then back again, like commuters, at the same hours in the morning and evening.

The peewit, or plover, will be doing dancing acrobatics in the air. In a few weeks time they will have their nests, a small depression in the ground lined with a few skimpy wisps of dried straw or grass. The simplicity helps as a camouflage against their many predators. Their voracity in consuming insects makes them a welcome ally to the farmer, and they came under the protection of an Act that prohibits killing them or taking their eggs. Plover eggs used to be collected and were so popular for food in restaurants and inns that the bird was disappearing from England. The sign of plovers flying south has always been an indicator to the farmer that a cold front with a freeze is on its way.

Twelfth Night on January 5th is the **Vigil of the Feast of Epiphany** and occurs on the eleventh night after Christmas. The practice of calling it Twelfth Night, instead of Twelfth Day's Eve comes from the Teutonic system of measuring time by nights rather than by days. Epiphany is from the Greek for appearance and celebrates the anniversary of Christ's manifestation to the three wise men. The twelve days between the Nativity on Christmas Day and Epiphany form the nucleus of the lengthy religious Christmas observances, which extend from Advent to Candlemas. In the West Midlands, **Twelfth Night fires** were lit in the wheat fields. It was traditional to have eleven small ones and a large one representative of Christ and his disciples. At some farms a thirteenth fire, symbolic of Judas Iscariot, was lit and then quickly smothered. As in the Burning of the Bush rite, there would be a gathering around the large fire, cider toasts and merrymaking followed by a festive supper at the farmhouse. In Hereford and Worcester, after the dinner, the **oxen** would be **wassailed** while toasts of ale were drunk. The beasts' good health would be required to draw the plough for the new year's planting.

The twelve days of Christmas were the medieval peasants' holiday from the fields and traditionally was enjoyed with revelry. Although the ecclesiastical Christmas season extends to Candlemas on February 2, Epiphany signified the end of the holidays for most people. In olden times, Christmas greenery was left up until Candlemas Eve, but today, the practice of partying and taking down the Christmas decorations at the end of these twelve days is our inheritance of this recognition that the holidays are over.

Merrymaking would reach its peak with the Twelfth Day's feast, the highlights of which were the **Twelfth Cake**, baked with a bean hidden in its interior. As this feast celebrated the Three Kings, the custom was to have a Mock King who would be master of the ceremonies, and who would be chosen randomly by being the one who received the bean in his slice of the Twelfth Cake. The King, in turn, would be able to pick his Queen. If a woman received the bean, she had the right to choose her King. Later on a pea was also hidden in the cake and its recipient would become the Queen of the Feast.

Twelfth Cakes, which were elaborately decorated, and of a sweet, dark consistency, have almost disappeared now in favour of the more popular Christmas Pudding. One of the few remaining ones is the Baddeley Cake which is enjoyed by actors at the Theatre Royal in Drury Lane every January 6th as a legacy of Richard Baddeley, a chef and actor, who left £100 for this purpose when he died in 1794.

Election of the King of the Bean

The twelve days of Christmas were holidays from the hard farming work of ploughing, fertilising the fields with manure and much of the other outdoor work. Women on the farms traditionally took a break from their spinning. These weren't complete holidays, though, as cows still had to be milked, wood for the fire chopped, any calving and lambing attended to, animals fed, and the usual chores of looking after the family and washing still had their daily cycles.

On **Ploughtide**, the first Sunday after Epiphany, the plough and farm workers are blessed at the church, for the next day, **Plough Monday**, or **St. Distaff's Day**, is the first of ploughing to initiate the New Year's cycle. Distaff was never the name of a saint. The name is attributed to a poem of Robert Herrick's, written in the seventeenth century:

Partly work and partly play
Ye must on St. Distaff's Day.
From the plough soon free the teame,
Then come home and fother them.
If the Maides a-spinning goe,
Burn the flax, and fire the tow.
Bring in pailes of water then,
Let the Maides bewash the men.
Gives St. Distaff all the right,
Then bid Christmas sport good night;
And next morrow every one,
To his own vocation.
Hesperides, Saint Distaff's Day, 1648

Distaff means 'Rock' and is the term used for the cleft stick upon which wool or flax was wound for spinning by hand. St. Distaff's Day inferred that the women, or distaff side of the house, were also expected to be making an end to the holidays by resuming their spinning.

Spinning with the Distaff

Plough Monday and St. Distaff's Day were more of a gradual easing back to work that a full day's drudgery. The day was generally celebrated as one of half work and half play. In some parts of England, **plough matches** gave it a festive air. More northerly counties had **sword-dancing** festivities, while the **Fool Plough procession** used to be an English tradition. Plough Boys would dress up as mummers and lead a decorated plough from door to door, asking for gifts of money. If they were refused, they would immediately set to and plough up the miserly resident's garden! Part of the monies thus collected would go to the Church and, until the Reformation, it was used to maintain the Plough Light, a candle lit before the Plough Guild's altar in the chantry of the church. Any money left over went toward a merry evening for the participants.

Procession of the Plough on Plough Monday

In some regions a **Corn Dolly**, or **Kern Baby**, was laid in the first furrow of the cornfield and the plough would carefully turn the earth over it to bury it as an offering to the Corn Goddess in hopes of a plentiful harvest. Such Dollies were made from the final stalks of corn cut in the last harvest, which had reverently been kept on the farmhouse hearth until this day.

The first ploughing usually has its complement in preparing the beds in the kitchen and market gardens with a shovel. Today, of course, the plough has all but disappeared with the advent of the tractor. Rooks used to follow the wending plough on its journey through the fields for the easy pickings of grubs and other insects revealed in the freshly turned earth. Now the noisy tractor keeps them away but, once it moves further away or leaves the field, they descend in a ragged formation for their feast, no doubt made all the more delicious from the waiting.

After the rich foods of enjoyed over Christmas and the twelve days' festivities, the farmer, with an eye to his rapidly expanding waistline and a fresh respect for the pitfalls of intoxicating beverages taken to excess, is glad to settle back by his hearth in the long quiet evenings, and to eat a more basic and regular fare of vegetables from his cold cellar and attic. Not too long ago, it was common for a large percentage of the populace to have meat only one day a week during such non-festive periods. Beetroot, parsnips, turnips, carrots, swedes and other root vegetables are staples. Well-stocked cellars are raided for their winter's hoard: sacks of potatoes, trays of apples and strings of onions.

In addition to the ploughing, January's absence of foliage and of a bright sun overhead make it easier for the farmer to get on with other necessary chores: clearing bracken and mangelwurzels, ditching to allow a flow of fresh water for both livestock and crops and cutting and clearing hedges, nettles, brambles and cow parsley. Any sturdy branches cut can be taken away to be used for stakes, while the rest will burn easily if there is not too much rain.

Through the centuries there has been an evolution of skills required on the farm for hedge cutting, thatching hayricks, ploughing and other chores, which have been learned through oral tradition and on-the-job understudying. These highly developed skills are rarely appreciated by the urban-dwellers who consume the rural produce. As an example, proper hedging of the traditional box, yew and privet requires a true craftsman, as well as the tools which have been specially designed for this purpose. First, dead branches and plants and any growth that doesn't contribute to the hedge are cleared out. The critical eye of an experienced hedge cutter will know which new long branches to leave, and these he partly cuts through and bends to interweave with either the existing hedge or newly laid stakes. These binding boughs, and their many shoots during the new season, give new life and added strength to the old hedge. A properly tended hedge will serve its master well by keeping the worst of the wind off his crops, containing his animals and acting as a boundary marker. Trees that develop in hedges used to be used in building houses, and hedge plants with edible produce helped to vary the fare for both the farmhouse kitchen and the local wildlife.

January in pastoral England is a time of preparing for lambing. In different regions of the country nursery pens will have been prepared, their floors strewn with dried straw, and hurdles set around them to keep the wind out. The first bleats of newly born lambs on a January night are age-old sign that a new year has begun. Before enclosures for lambing came into common usage, the earliest lambs born in January were often kept in the kitchen, warm and coddled, to ensure their survival. Sheep farming was not so much a commercial endeavour directed at the marketplace until railways and factories came into existence. Sheep used to be kept as a way of life in rural England in order that the household be self-sufficient. They gave milk for a few weeks after weaning their lambs, wool which was homespun into cloth, and precious meat for the table. The ancient and enduring popularity of the Twenty-third Psalm, "The Lord is My Shepherd," reminds us of the esteem in which sheep were held and cared for through the ages.

One of England's most traditional folk-customs that occurs in January is that of **wassailing**, or toasting the health of **apple orchards** and cider drinkers on January 16. Wassailing orchards is actually a Twelfth Night ceremony, but the timing is still based on the old Julian Calendar, which fixes Christmas on January 5 and Epiphany on the 17th, eleven days after the feast days designated by the Gregorian Calendar. Although the Julian Calendar allowed for leap years to take care of the fraction of a day not accounted for in the 365-day year when it was implemented in the 7th century, B.C., this still involved some rounding, which made the calendar out by three days every 400 years. The error that crept in amounted to ten days by the time Pope Gregory XIII made the correction in 1582 by dropping those days and introducing the rule that every century that was not divisible by 400 would not be a leap year. While Catholic countries and most of Europe adjusted their calendars accordingly, Protestant England refused to follow suit until 1752, by which time the error in the English calendar amounted to eleven days. The loss of eleven days gave rise to consternation in the farm folk, who were now confused as to which date was proper for their festivities. Relaying more on nature's calendar than the legal one, crowds assembled at Glastonbury to see which day the Holy Thorn would bloom, tradition being that it always bloomed on the anniversary of Christ's Nativity. Since the first blossoms emerged January 5, 1752, many people in the West Country believed that to be the true Christmas. That naturally made the proper Twelfth Night January 16, and it has been the customary night for Wassailing every since. Strictly speaking, though, the Wassailers have by now fallen between the two calendars. Had they wished to be true to the old Julian one, they would have to add a day each for 1800 and 1900, for the error in the Julian calendar would presently amount to thirteen days.

The celebrants prepare a Wassail Punch called "Lamb's Wool," usually a hot concoction of cider or ale with spices, sugar and roasted apples and drink it around a roaring bonfire in the apple orchards.

According to one authority, the name derives from November 1 having been dedicated to the saint responsible for fruit and seeds. That day became known as *La Mas Ubhal*, the day of the apple, which sounded like "Lamasool," and was eventually corrupted to "Lamb's Wool," the drink enjoyed on All Hallow's Eve and on Twelfth Night. It is an appropriate name, for the roast apples burst and float on the top of the punch, giving the appearance of virgin wool.

Cider is poured around the trunks of the trees, and sometimes pieces of cider soaked bread are wedged into the branches. A volley of shot from old rifles is fired through the branches and a Wassailing song is sung by all to the accompaniment of music played by a rustic band. The firing of the guns may be a method of frightening evil spirits away, but more likely was originally meant to wake the apple tree up for another fruitful year.

There are many variants of Wassailing songs, but a typical one reported in *The Gentleman's Magazine* in 1791 is:

> Here's to thee old apple-tree
> Whence thou may'st bud, and when though may'st blow!
> And whence thou may'st bear apples enow!
> Hatsfull! Capsfull!
> Bushel-bushel-sacksfull,
> And my pockets full too! Huzza!

A related custom involved Visiting Wassailers carrying a decorated Wassail Bowl, usually wooden, from house to house during the Twelve Days of Christmas, and offering to sing a Wassail Song for the benefit of the household or its orchards. In return they would expect gifts of money, food or drink. There are minor variants to the song, but a usual one is:

> Wassail! Wassail! All over the town!
> Our toast is white, our ale is brown;
> Our bowl is made of the maplin tree,
> We be good fellows, I drink to thee.

Early accounts indicate that they started out with a bowl full of drink and would gradually empty it through the course of the evening. Later on, an empty bowl was taken round in hopes it would be filled at each house.

It was natural for animals to bear their young in the spring, when food in the fields would be available. Calving was no exception, though early calves would begin arriving in January, especially now that the farmer ensures his cows are fed through the winter. January would see the opening of the old thatched hayricks to provide fodder. Mangelwurzel, or field beets, used to be planted for feeding cattle and ewes in lamb in January, as it would reach its prime after Christmas, when other grass crops were dead. The farmer would have to cut swedes and mangels for his cattle. This was pretty much replaced by kale which, although requiring more preparation of the land, can be eaten straight from the fields and has the added advantage of providing cover for pheasants and partridge for the January sportsmen. Later on in the month, there also used to be a bustling and colour in the rural villages in the readying for the meetings of the foxhound packs.

Weather is a critical factor, not only to today's farmer, but to farmers of all ages. A poor harvest could result in famine during the ensuing winter in the not very distant past. As a consequence, a wealth of weather lore has grown up in the country. Perhaps we should be grateful for a cold first month, as gloomy proverbs warn against a balmy one:

> March in Janiveer,
> Janiveer in March, I fear.

And

> If January calends be summerly gay,
> Twill be winterly weather till the calends of May.

St. Vincent's Day on January 22 and **St. Paul's Conversion Day** on the 25th are both considered indicators of the coming year's weather. Good, sunny weather will bring a prosperous harvest, while storms and wind herald ill-fortune.

FEBRUARY

All the months in the year
Curse a fair Februeer

Verstegan has written that the Saxons named this month *Sproutkale*, due to the prominence on cabbage sprouting against a backdrop of so much barrenness that is associated with this time of year. Later on, they called it *Sol-monatt*, honouring the longer daylight that came from the returning sun. Symbolically, February used to be represented as a man in a sky-coloured dress, holding in his hand the astrological sign Pisces, whose reign begins towards the end of this month.

Numa Pompilius, King of Rome in the seventh century, B.C., introduced February as a month at the same time he did January. In Latin, *Februare* means to purify, and the month's name derived from *Februa*, the Roman festival of purification and expiation observed annually at this time. The earlier Romulus year had contained only 304 days, while Numa's new year was 355 in length, so as to be more consistent with the lunar calendar. February was originally placed after December and was to be the end of the year, while the other new month, January, was set as the beginning of the new annual calendar. In 452 B.C., the positions of January and February were reversed to the order we now know them in. Numa also made February the shortest month, giving it 29 days on every regular year and 30 every fourth, or leap, year. Later on, Augustus Caesar shortened it even further by stealing a day from February, and adding it to August, so that the month named for him would have 31 days, and thus would not be outdone by those other months which had already possessed that many (notably July, which had been named for Julius Caesar).

Weatherwise, England's February still sees some frost and snow, and is only a slight improvement over January. It is characterised by its windy days and lots of rain and flooding, but also by occasional spells of a few warmer, clear days which allow the snowdrop and early crocus to push their way out of the earth and raise false expectations of an early spring. Even the end of the month may greet us with frost, sleet and snow. Its fickle weather is reflected in the rural proverb

> February fill the dyke
> Either with the black or white.

It almost seems that February's poor weather inheritance of less days than any other month was the ancient's way of saying that the sooner it was over the better.

Although most of the urban English today associate February with colds, coughs and a bout of the flu, our country forefathers endowed with a rich share of customs and festivities. February 1 figured prominently in the ancient Celtic pastoral calendar as one of the four major annual feast days. They called it *Imbolc*, to celebrate their lambing festival, and enjoyed a pagan Feast of Lights. Lambing was arranged at this time, as it still is today on many farms, so that the animals would be old enough to begin grazing when the grass is sufficiently developed in the spring, and later large enough to fetch the best prices in the early summer markets.

For the farmer's wife, February was when the cade lambs, those over and above what the ewe could feed, would be kept in the back kitchen and handfed their milk, after waking the household early every morning with their hungry bleats. These endearing little creatures would often acquire names from the children and become such established members of the household that serious grief would strike when the time came for marketing the pets. During the month, the lambs and ewes out on the hills and downs find dwindling nourishment and must be fed extra rations. The poor shepherds would have to stay out in the pastures to care for them. Otherwise many would be lost.

The first of February has more recently been associated through Christianity as being **Candlemas Eve**. Candlemas, being the fortieth day of Christmas, draws a close to the long ecclesiastical Christmas celebrations that began with Advent. Candlemas Eve was the date for ensuring all Christmas decorations and greenery be taken out of the churches, and oatcakes were customarily eaten afterwards. Robert Herrick spoke of this day in some of his renowned lines from *"Hesperides, Ceremony for Candlemas Eve"* written in 1648:

> Down with the rosemary and bays,
> Down with the mistletoe,
> Instead of holly now upraise
> The greener box for show.
>
> The holly hitherto did sway,
> Let box now domineer,
> Until the dancing Easter day
> Or Easter's eve appear.

There was a superstition that bad luck would follow for those who hadn't thoroughly removed their greenery, and wealthier folk would send their servants to sweep out their private pews, ensuring not a single stray leaf remained. Herrick plays on this theme with this poetic admonition:

> That so the superstitions find
> No one least branch left there behind;
> For look how many leaves there be
> Neglected there, maids trust to me,
> So many goblins you shall see!

Candlemas itself, Febuary 2, is a double feast day which commemorates the Purification of the Blessed Virgin Mary, when Mary was ritually cleansed in the Temple after the birth of Christ, as well as the anniversary of the Presentation of Christ in the Temple. It seems to be no coincidence that the early Roman association of February with purification was later adopted by the Christian fathers. The lovely white snowdrop has been called the purification flower, as it blooms around the date of this celebration.

The association of Candlemas with lights may derive from the pre-Christian pagan **Feast of Lights** celebrated during the Celtic lambing festival, and may also have some connection with the Roman Lupercalia, which was observed in mid-February. The name Candlemas comes from the practice since the 5th century of consecrating candles in the churches and passing them out to the congregations, and is also associated with the penitential processions carrying wax candles or tapers in Rome. The act of **candle bearing** on this date is supposed to derive from Simeon's words in Luke 2:32, on taking the baby Jesus in his arms when Mary was purified, that the Christ child was "A light to lighten the Gentiles, and the glory of thy people Israel."

In Catholic England, before the Reformation, there was a belief prevalent that the bigger and brighter the candle, the more curative protection it would give its carrier in the processions, as well as safeguard against storms and earthquakes. This superstition is illustrated in a Candlemas verse from Barnaby Googe's Translation of Naogeorgus in the *Popish Kingdom* (quoted from Ellis's Edition of Brand's *Observations on the Popular Antiquities of Great Britain*):

> This done, each man his candle lights,
> Where chiefest seemest he,
> Whose taper may be greatest seen;
> And fortunate to be,
> Whose candle burneth clear and bright:
> A wondrous force and might
> Doth in these candles lie, which if
> At any time they light,
> They sure believe that neither storm
> Nor tempest doth abide,
> Nor thunder in the skies be heard,
> Nor any devil's spide,
> Nor fearful sprites that walk by night,
> Nor hurts of frost or hail, (etc.)

The name **Candlemas** is also affiliated with a general belief in England that now that the sun is gradually rising in the horizon, by February 2, daylight has increased to the point where significantly less lighting up time, or candlelight, is required. The country proverb, "On Candlemas Day throw candles away," implies this, but may have more reference to the Christmas season being over and a putting away of the festive Christmas candles.

There is a custom of **Cradle-rocking**, reminiscent of Christ in the Temple, which takes place annually on the closest Sunday to February 2 at Blidworth, Nottinghamshire. The last male child baptised before this date in the parish, and preferably the first-born in a family, is placed by the Vicar into a lovely old wooden cradle on rockers, decoratively painted with flowers and leaves, set near the altar. The cradle is then rocked about a dozen times and, after prayers, the child is removed from it and returned to its parents while the *Nunc Dimittis* is sung by the choir. This re-enactment of the Presentation used to be part of medieval miracle plays, and local tradition affirms that this was a practice in the parish since the 13th century. Although it stopped after the Reformation, it was reinstated in 1923 and has since been an annual event.

In line with the name Candlemas and the Presentation of our Lord in the Temple, it used to be a practice for a mother to carry candles to the church after she had given birth; and, possibly for this reason, in the north of England Candlemas is known as **Wives' Feast Day**. This custom of mothers being purified after giving birth used to be known as 'churching,' or 'being churched.'

As on Paul's Conversion Day just over a week before, Candlemas weather has traditionally been held as prophetic of the year to come. A warm and sunny Candlemas Day is supposed to presage an extended winter and poor harvest but, if it is a day of bad weather, luck will be better. A saying in Northern England and Scotland goes:

> If Candlemas Day be dry and fair,
> The half of winter's to come and mair;
> If Candlemas Day be wet and foul,
> The half of winter's gane at Yule.

And

> If Candlemas be fair and clear,
> We'll have two winters in one year.

The badger and groundhog, friends to English nature-lovers, figure similarly in popular German and American lore on Candlemas. The German saying, "The badger peeps out of his hole on Candlemas Day and, if he finds snow, he walks abroad; but, if he sees the sun shining, he draws back into his hole" implies, as in American Groundhog Day tradition, that a sunny February 2 will bring a longer winter for everyone and send the weatherwise animals back into hiberbation.

For our ancestors, whose well-being often depended on their self-sufficiency, Candlemas was an important milestone in the traditional long and dreary winter. The proverb,

> A farmer should on Candlemas Day
> Have half his corn and half his hay

infers that, in a well-managed household, the farmer should have half his winter's fodder and half of his stores for his own table left to see his livestock and family through until the first crops would be ready.

The next day, February 3, is the **Feast of St. Blaise**, patron saint of both wool-combers and those who have illnesses of the throat. St. Blaise was a doctor who later held the position of Bishop of Sebaste in Armenia, where he was martyred in 316. Blaise was a forerunner of St. Francis of Assissi, as he was reputed to have a great love for, and power over, both wild and domesticated animals. There is a story that, when he was captured by the troops of Lucinius and was being led to his imprisonment, he saved a boy who was choking to death on a fishbone by touching the boy's throat. The ceremony of **Blessing the Throat** is still celebrated at some English Roman Catholic churches on this Saint's feast day. Chambers, writing in 1863, says, *"In the simple days when England was Catholic, it was believed that, by a charm in the name of St. Blaise, a bone could be extracted from the throat, or a thorn from the flesh. It was only necessary to hold the patient and say, 'Blaize, the martyr and servant of Jesus Christ, commands thee (in the case of a bone in the throat) to pass up or down; (in the case of a thorn) to come forth'; and the command was instantly effectual."*

Later, before he was beheaded in his martyrdom, St. Blaise's flesh was torn with iron combs, similar to those used in cloth-making in the wool industry. For this reason, wool-combers and others in the wool trade adopted him as their patron saint. Up until the end of the first quarter of the nineteenth century, his feast day was celebrated with spectacular pageantry and **processions in wool towns**. All who were involved with wool and its processing, from simple shepherds to prosperous merchants, would participate. The processions, led by a man representing St. Blaise, along with speeches and other festivities, would draw visitors from far and near. Possibly because its date is so near to that of Candlemas, or perhaps because some took the word 'blaze' to be a word play on 'Blaise', some other parishes in England used to celebrate this feast day with large bonfires set up on the downs above their villages.

Another noticeable feature of England's February is the resurgence observed in the activities and sounds of birds. The blackbird and thrush can be seen singing in the blackthorn, which is beginning to blossom, sparrows chatter and the redbreast warns off his territorial boundaries. Chaffinches begin to be heard and seen, sporting a new spring plumage. House sparrows and ravens start building new nests in February, and rooks return to and refurbish their old ones.

Both the field mouse and squirrel wake from their winter's sleep with February's few warmer days. They munch at their harvest stores and then, when the weather takes a turn again for the worse – as it invariably does this month -, they curl up in their warm nests and go back to sleep. Similarly, while the 'false' sun brings out many more birds who make what meal they can out of the remainder of the winter garden, snow and cold soon send them back into hiding. Birds seem to sleep more at this time of year, providently requiring less food than when they are readying for their mating and nest-building.

Since at least as early as Chaucer, there has been a country tradition that birds choose their mates on February 14. This has romantically been linked with people also choosing a mate, or discovering - by a variety of means -, the identity of their future spouse. In fact, **Valentine customs** go back to the pagan Roman festival of fertility, *Lupercalia*, honouring the Lycaean Pan, which included choosing partners by lots, and a ritual sacrifice of animals. There are reputed to have been two St. Valentines; one was a Roman priest who was believed to have been beheaded on the Flamian Way in 269 AD, and the other was an Umbrian bishop, who is thought to have met a similar fate in 273. While these may have been the same man, little is known about either, and their real stories are shrouded in the mists of time. Both, however, are said to have died on February 14, the eve of Lupercalia. There is a legend that the gaol-keeper's daughter fell in love with one of them, and that, on the morning of his execution, he left her a poignant note signed simply, 'Your Valentine'. Other than this simple note, and the time of year he was martyred in, there seems to be no logical reason for which St. Valentine has become such a popular friend and patron of lovers. The crocus, which blooms at this time, with an early promise of spring to come, has been dedicated to him.

Although the early Christian fathers tried hard to eradicate the pagan customs of choosing a partner by lots for the next year, the tradition did not die easily. In England, lots were still drawn up until the eighteenth century as a method of discovering one's sweetheart. In some places, lots were drawn three times, and if one received the same name each time, it was taken to be a sure sign that a marriage would be forthcoming.

Valentine customs have generally been more popular with girls, and a variety of practices, such as putting a bay leaf under the pillow, or wearing one's socks inside out on Valentine's Eve, were believed to bring a dream of one's future husband.

Another custom, still popular in some parts, was a belief that one's Valentine would be the first member of the opposite gender one saw on February 14. This resulted in some amusing precautions having to be taken to avoid being saddled with an undesirable partner. Pepys notes in his diary for February 14, 1662, that his wife had to cover her eyes during the morning until her chosen Valentine arrived, to avoid seeing any of the workmen who were gilding their chimney that day. In those days it was practice for married people to have Valentines other than their spouses. An exchange of presents between Valentines used to be even more popular than the same at Christmas, and Pepys notes that wealthier people outdid each other in giving valuable, albeit ostentatious, Valentine gifts.

In more rural parts of England, children would use the occasion for another excursion around the neighbourhood, reciting a short verse at doors and expecting to be given sweets, fruit or a few pennies. One popular version was:
> Good morrow, Valentine
> Change your luck and I'll change mine
> We are raggety, you are fine,

So, pray give us a Valentine.

In some districts the children would be rewarded with a Valentine Bun, also known as a Plum Shuttle, made with currents or caraway seeds, in the form of weaver's shuttle.

St Valentine's letter shower

The practice of giving elaborate Valentine gifts began to die out in the late eighteenth century, and was gradually replaced with the Valentine cards we know so well today. The earliest ones were handmade, but commercial printers soon saw a profit in it, and began producing and selling great quantities of cards in the mid-nineteenth century. During the hey-day of Valentines in the late 1800s, considerable extra staff would have to be taken on at Post Offices to handle the heavy volume of Valentine mail.

Another unrelated custom which takes place on February 14 is the **Blessing of the Salmon-Net Fisheries** at Norham-on-Tweed, Northumberland, honouring the commencement of their fishing season. Just before midnight, the Vicar holds a well-attended open air service, blessing the fisheries, boats, nets, fishermen and the river itself. After the service, the first boat sets out to begin the news season. Although this service is only about a century old, local tradition believes it to be rooted in ancient similar rituals common to fishermen everywhere.

February 14 is also the beginning of the ancient six-day **Mart at King's Lynn**, Norfolk. This is one of only five fairs in all of Britain which are called Marts, and its original charter dates from the eleventh century. By attracting visitors and promoting sales of locally made goods, fairs were of vital economic importance to early communities. Except for interruptions during two world wars and the Great Plague of 1666, King's Lynne Mart has been operating continuously for over 700 years. It is still opened annually with a procession from the Guildhall to the Market Place, where the Mayor, dressed in scarlet robes, reads the ancient Proclamation. A more recent tradition associated with the opening day's festivities has been to reserve the first ride on the roundabout for the Mayor and the other members of the Corporation.

February is a busy month for the farmer. More outside work can be accomplished due to the longer and slightly warmer days. Fortunately, the farmer likes a wet February, as is attested to in an English saying about the Welsh:
    The Welshman would rather see his dam on her bier,
    Than see a fair Februeer.

The ducks and geese love it, too, as do seagulls who come inland to some parts for the winter. With the melting snow and rain, the dykes (ditches) overflow, flooding the fields and enriching them with silt. The ground is saturated and waterlogged and, in some areas, the flooding gives the landscape a complete change in appearance, with only the tips of the hedgerows visible above the water. At these times, the cattle are moved to higher ground, and the hedgerows become sanctuaries for mice, weasels and other animals. Later in the dry summer, the lower-lying parts of the fields will sport a greener grass to show where these miniature lakes and ponds were.

Ditching and ploughing are important parts of the farmer's February cycle. The first ploughing is done on the highest ground, which dries first. A watchful eye will be kept on the maintenance of the hayricks, which had been opened in January, as they have to withstand the elements through March to keep the livestock fed.

Throughout February the farmers traditionally brought their sacks of corn to the mills, to be ground up for flour, barley meal and bran. Some of this they would take home for their own kitchens and livestock. The rest they would sell to the miller, who would grind it and sell it to others for a profit. The old mills used to be water and wind-powered. Later steam engines were added, so that they could operate at any time, without being dependent on the state of the winds or rivers.

Barley and wheat will have been planted and, where needed, a scarecrow is erected to help ensure the early planting has not been in vain. Potatoes, a British crop only since about 1750, are sorted for those to eat and those to keep for planting. Not so long ago in England, before imported foods became common, the winter fare of vegetables would acquire a quality of interminable monotony during February. Meals would revolve around a cycle of beetroot, cabbage, kale, leeks, parsnips, swedes, turnips and the last (and worst) of the Brussels sprouts and winter apples. With palates longing for a change, there was an extra incentive for the farmer to ensure as early a planting as possible.

Part of the lore in planting is mysteriously connected with the moon. Peas and beans traditionally had to be sown during a waning moon, while all other seeds during a waxing one, even though there appears no scientific reason. It is, however, common knowledge that the moon has a gravitational effect on tides as well as on all other water on our planet, with the strongest pull occurring at the time of the full moon. It was believed that seeds planted during a waxing moon would germinate and grow in sympathetic correspondence. This logic has never been scientifically disproved, and certainly seems to have worked over the centuries. But no satisfactory explanation has been put forward on the reasons for planting peas and beans when the moon is waning.

Subject to climate variations at different parts of England, there are varying dates for the proverbs which remind the farmer to busy himself with his planting. The earliest, for where it is warmest first, is on the second:

> Set beans in Candlemas waddle.

For other parts it is on the 14th:

> On Valentine's set thy hopper by mine.

Still later, others would begin on St. Matthias's feast day:

> On St. Matthio, take thy hopper and sow.

St. Matthias is mentioned only briefly at the end of the first chapter of the Acts of Apostles as being elected one of the apostles to replace Judas. Little is known about Matthias's later career, and it is thought he suffered martyrdom in either Palestine or Ethiopia. Another St, Matthias day saying heralds the coming of the English spring:

> St. Matthee sends the sap up the tree.

Every four years, with the exception of three century marks out of four, brings a leap year day at the end of February. The reason for this is that the Equinoctial, or Tropical, Year is actually 365.242199 days long, measuring the time required for a complete revolution of the sun from equinox to equinox. The extra fraction, almost one-quarter of a day, has been adjusted for with the leap year day since the sixth century. It is customary for those born on this day to celebrate their birthdays on February 28 in Common, or non-leap, years. February 29 is the feast day of **St. Oswald of Worcester**, who died on this day in 992. While he is the only saint to have ever had February 29th, his feast day has traditionally been observed on the 28th since the 1930s.

There are varying stories connected with the origin of the term 'leap year'. The most common one derives from the early practice of putting the extra day with the one preceding it, and calling them both the same date, thereby minimising any confusion to the rustic calendar by 'leaping over' the additional day.

MARCH

March in Janiveer,
Janiveer in March, I fear.

March was known as *Rhedmonath* by the Saxons, after either their diety Rheda – to whom they sacrificed in this month -, or the Saxon word *raed*, meaning council, as this was usually the time of the Gothic council meetings, which were held before expeditions and wars. They also called it *Elydmonath*, after the word *Elyd*, for 'stormy', a reflection on the high blustery March winds which we still know today. Later, according to Verstegan, March was known as *Lenct-monat*, meaning 'length month', or 'spring', due to the ever-lengthening days which, during this month, first begin to be longer than the nights. Since the Christian custom of fasting, which has been observed by them at this time of year, fell mostly within this month - and partially during the preceding and/or ensuing month, it became known as the fast of *Lenct,* which was later shortened to Lent.

As in other months, our present name for March is Roman in origin. This was their first month of the year, called *Martius*, dedicated to their God of war, Mars, whom they also believed was father to their founder Romulus. The symbol for March was a dark and fierce-countenanced man with a war helmet on his head. He is depicted with a spade and holds a basket of seeds on his arm, a spray of almond blossoms in his left hand and the sign of Aries, the Ram, in his right.

Like the Romans, the Israelites also observed March as the beginning of their sacred year, because of the divine commandment in Exodus 12:1 and 2: "And the Lord spake unto Moses and Aaron in the land of Egypt, saying, This month shall be unto you the beginning of months: It shall be the first month of the year to you." Similarly, until September 1752, the English civil, or legal, year did not begin until Lady Day, or the Day of Annunciation, March 25, although the historical or popular year had started on January 1st.

The weather in March is characterised by great changes from which is derived the saying, 'March comes in like a lion, but goes out like a lamb; but, if it comes in like a lamb, it goes out like a lion.'

It is a relatively dry month of swelling buds, chilling blasts of winds and some warm days which do not last. The dryness clears up the last of February's flooding, and prevents the newly planted seeds from rotting in the ground. The cold winds conspire to keep the seeds from opening and sprouting too far, protecting them from the last lingering effects of winter.

Another characteristic of March, which is now almost a memory, was the maintenance of the thatched roofs. It used to be a common sight in rural England to see cottagers, awakened from their sleepy Sunday hearths, swarming up ladders set against their dwellings, to repair the damage done to their thatch by the March winds.

We begin to see some colourful variety in the gardens and fields. Crocuses push their heads above the ground and primroses begin to peer out from the hedges. One of the prettiest of English flowers, the wild daffodil, can be seen bravely nodding in the cold winds, while there are an abundance of violets, which Shakespeare called 'sweeter than the lids of Juno's eyes', hugging the ground in sheltered spots and making themselves known mostly by their fragrance.

There used to be a country proverb that spring had not truly arrived until you could plant you foot upon nine daisies. The daisy is one of the earliest recorded English flowers, still called by its Saxon name, meaning 'day's eye' or 'eye-of-day'. Chaucer describes how he would go out early in the morning, and then again in the evening, first to see the day's eye unfold, and then to watch it shut back up again for the night.

The month of March, as well as many of its individual customs and festivals, has since ancient times been tied to the Christian Church's observance of **Lent**, in remembrance of Jesus' 40 days of miraculous fasting. The timing of Lent is not fixed to a specific date in our annual calendar, but depends upon the important moveable feast of Easter. In order to settle internal controversy in the early Christian church,

Constantine decreed at the Council of Nicaea (A.D. 325) that Easter would be celebrated on the first Sunday following the first full moon occurring after March 21st. If that full moon came on a Sunday, Easter Day would be the Sunday after. Easter, then, depends on both the full moon and on March 21st, which Constantine reckoned should always be considered the vernal equinox. The earliest date for Easter is March 22, when March 21 is a Saturday on which the full moon occurs. The latest date for Easter is April 25.

Easter and Christmas are the keys for fixing the dates of the other moveable feasts and fasts throughout the Christian year. Consulting the table of '*Lessons Proper for Sundays*' in any *Book of Common Prayer of the Church of England*, it can be seen, for example, that the nine Sundays preceding Easter, which include those which usually dominate the month of March, are Septuagesima, Sexagesima and Quinquagesima Sundays (meaning, respectively, that they occur about 70, 60 and 50 days before Easter) and the six Sundays of Lent.

Lent itself encompasses a period of 46 days, because the Sundays which occur within it were considered improper for fasting. This leaves a remainder of the 40 Biblical days of abstinence. Lent may begin on the 4th of February at the earliest, and on the 10th of March at the latest. Timed as it generally is to cover the period extending from late February to early April, Lent occurs during what is indubitably the leanest period of the year. For our recent rural ancestors, winter supplies from the last harvest would be dwindling, while those from the new year's crops would not yet be available. If the previous autumn's harvest had been a poor one, there would have been no choice *but* to fast during this period, with or without the associated church-sanctioned virtues of Lent. Even in current experience in urban England, when imported 'fresh' fruit and vegetables are more generally available during this and other months, March stands out in many housewives' minds as the month commanding the combination of some of the highest prices with the least variety of such fresh foods. Locally produced root vegetables are on the wane, although beetroot, carrots, swedes and leeks are available, along with the worst of the parsnips and turnips. One can still find local broccoli, cabbage and rhubarb for sale, as well as the last of the apples and pears, but new greens are required for the table, and watercress, spring onions and cauliflower begin appearing toward the end of the month.

The first day of the long fast of Lent is **Ash Wednesday**, and so - naturally preceding this – there had to be some feasting and merry-making in order to use up and enjoy those foods remaining in the larder which would be forbidden during Lent. This license to 'eat, drink and be merry' was exercised during **Shrovetide**, the period encompassing the four days preceding Ash Wednesday. These days were known as Egg Saturday, Quinquagesima Sunday, Shrove or Collop Monday and Shrove Tuesday.

Shrove Tuesday comes from the Roman Catholic practice of confessing sins and being 'shrove', or 'shriven'. Absolution thus obtained, one could enter into Lent with a clean conscience, using the period both as a sort of penance for sins confessed to, and for the further purification of soul and body.

The four days of Shrovetide have different names, depending on the varying English counties they were observed in, and on the traditional foods they were celebrated with. Usually all fresh and salted meat had to be used up before Lent, as it was strictly forbidden. Often eggs, butter and lard were also banned. The meat would be eaten as collops, salted meat and eggs, for dinner on Collop Monday, and the eggs and butter would be used up in pancakes on Shrove Tuesday, now more commonly known as **Pancake Day**.

Early on the morning of Shrove Tuesday, before the Reformation, the parish church bell would ring out to remind one and all of the day's required confession and the need to be shriven. Even after the establishment of Protestantism in England, some parishes continued to ring this bell, but the solemn Roman Catholic purpose of it was dropped, and it became known as the Pancake Bell.

An account of the gluttonous carnival-like atmosphere of Shrove Tuesday, given by John Taylor, the water poet, in 1617, is quoted in the 1854 edition of *Howitt's Pictorial Calendar of the Seasons*:

> '*Shrove Tuesday*, at whose entrance in the morning all the whole kingdom is quiet, but by the time the clock strikes eleven --- which by the help of a knavish sexton is commonly before

nine, --- then there is a bell rung called the *Pancake Bell*, the sound whereof makes thousands of people distracted and forgetful either of manner or humanitie. Then there is a thing cal'd wheaten flowrs, which the sulphory, necromanticke cookes doe mingle with water, eggs, spice and other tragicall, magicall inchantments, and then they put it little by little into a frying pan of boyling suet, where it makes a confused dismal hissing --- like the Lernian snakes in the reeds of Acheron, Stix, or Phlegeton, --- until at last by the skill of the cooke it is transformed into the forme of a Flap-Jack, which in our translation is called a pancake, which ominous incantation the ignorant people doe devoure very greedily --- having for the most part well dined before --- but they have no sooner swallowed the sweet candied baite, but straight their wits forsake them, and they run starke mad, assembling in routs and throngs numberless of ungovernable numbers, with uncivill civill commotions.'

'Uncivill commotions' occurring in earlier days during Shrovetide included **cock-fighting** and **'thrashing the hen'**. Fortunately, the cruel sport of cock-fighting was eventually made a misdemeanour and legally punishable by a penalty. The players in the equally deplorable custom of thrashing the hen consisted of one fellow with a live hen and horse-bells tied to his back, and several other fellows, who were blindfolded and wielding heavy sticks. The latter would follow the sounds of the horse-bells, and endeavour to kill the hen with their sticks, meanwhile invariably hitting the man carrying it and each other in the attempt. The one who was successful in killing it would win it as a reward to enjoy with his pancake feast.

'Throwing at cocks' was another brutal, but popular, Shrovetide amusement up until the eighteenth century. The owner of a cock would tie it to a stake, usually at the local grammar school, and offer, for the price of two pence, three throws, or *shies*, at it with a broomstick from a distance of about 20 yards. The dead cock would be rewarded to the man or boy who had killed it with his throw.

'Lent Crocking', or **'Lentsharding'**, was also practiced much more recently in some of England's counties, most notably in the Southwest. Gangs of youths would wander from door to door, after

having armed themselves with broken crockery. The leader would
approach the door and demand food or drink, usually with a verse
such as the following one given in *Chamber's Book of Days*:

> A-shrovin, a-shrovin,
> I be come a-shrovin;
> A piece of bread, a piece of cheese,
> A bit of your fat bacon,
> Or a dish of of your own makin!
>
> A-shrovin, a-shrovin,
> I be come a-shrovin,
> Nice meat in a pie,
> My mouth is very dry!
> I wish I was zoo well-a-wet
> I'de zing the louder for a nut!
>
> *Chorus:* A-shrovin, a-shrovin,
> We be come a shrovin!

If alms in the form of food and drink were not immediately
forthcoming, the leader would give the signal to his motley crew, who
would bombard the door with their shards of crockery. The more
unruly ones would attack it with stones, hammers and brickbats.

Although **Shrovetide alms processions** used to be a method for the
poorer members of the community to benefit from their wealthier
neighbours, Shroving more recently evolved into a children's outing
with less threatening verses, such as the following one from the
Southwest being employed:

> Tippety-tippety-tin
> Give me a pancake and I'll come in.
> Tippety-tippety-toe,
> Give me a pancake and then I'll go.

Another very popular Shrovetide custom was **hurling**, a sort of free-
for-all street football played with little or no formal rules. This was
enjoyed in places as widespread as Chester-le-Street (Durham),

London, St. Ives (Cornwall), and Workington (Cumbria). The locals entered into the spirit of hurling with such abandon that windows along the street would be barricaded, and contestants would take recesses from the game to settle disputes among themselves with their fists. The mayhem grew to such degrees in some locations that the authorities, constables – and even soldiers -, would be called to maintain the peace. The game was banned and discontinued in many towns, but a less violent version is still practiced today in others.

Our most common association with Shrove Tuesday is that of making and eating pancakes. The day used to be regionally called 'Fastern's e'en', being the eve of Lent but, for many in England, it is mostly enjoyed as Pancake Day – with **pancake races** and tossing -, while the pious Christian reasons for the custom are largely forgotten or ignored.

The ban on eggs during Lent may have also been an early method of securing an adequate crop of Easter chickens were hatched, and that thus a comfortable supply of both poultry and eggs be maintained for the rest of the year.

Throwing the pancakes at Westminster School

The oldest pancake race in England is reputed to be that run in Olney, Buckinghamshire, where it is claimed to date back to 1445. In the practice, the local church bell is rung twice, the first time to advise the local housewives to prepare their pancakes, and the second time to call them to the village square, wearing aprons and a head covering, and each carrying their pancake in a frying pan. Once they are assembled, the Pancake Bell rings, and they race from the square to the parish church, a distance of just under a quarter of a mile. The pancake must be tossed at the beginning and at the finish, and the winner is required to toss it one more time. If it falls to the ground, it may be picked up and tossed again. The first one reaching the church door wins a blessing from the Vicar and a Kiss of Peace from the Verger.

The next day, **Ash Wednesday**, is the first of Lent, and used to put an end to the Shrovetide antics, with the beginning of a solemn commemoration of Jesus' forty days of temptation and fasting in the wilderness. These forty days traditionally commenced on the first of six Sundays in Lent, and would lead up to Easter Day, the most important of the year's Christian celebrations. However, on the principle that Sundays should not be considered proper for fasting, and –if these are removed -, only thirty-six days of abstinence remain. For this reason, Pope Gregory moved the commencement of Lent back four days to Wednesday.

The name for Ash Wednesday comes from the ancient Roman Catholic ceremonial method of advising parishioners to "Remember, O man, that thou art dust, and to dust shalt return." The priest would thus admonish his parishioners while he drew the sign of the cross on the penitent's forehead with ashes made from the palms which had been consecrated on the previous Palm Sunday, the sixth Sunday of the prior year's Lent.

Although the observance of Lent became an established practice of the Christian Church as early as the fourth century, ashes were used in earlier Jewish tradition. In the Old Testament, ashes were symbolic of mortality, worthlessness, sorrow and repentance. While the sign of wearing the ashes on the forehead on Ash Wednesday did not become universal until the Synod of Benevento in 1091, history shows that Anglo-Saxon believers had already been practicing this a century before.

Ash Wednesday is still observed by Roman Catholics around the world and, in a slightly altered form, it survived the English Reformation for a short while as one of the ordinances of the Reformed Church until it was abandoned around 1547. Brand tells us in his *Observations on Popular Antiquities* that the day still continued to be one observed by the Church of England, but was used as an occasion for public readings which denounced recalcitrant sinners with curses.

Another popular Ash Wednesday custom which developed was the **"Jack-a-Lent"**, a scare-crow figure, at which boys would throw sticks, somewhat reminiscent of the poor cock they had "shied" at the day before.

Marble season, which heralded the coming spring, and was once a rather solemn sport indulged in by adults and children alike, would start on Ash Wednesday, and run until a serious championship match would be staged on Good Friday.

March 1 is the first fixed feast day in the month, and is celebrated as **St. David's Day**, a day when it used to be customary in some parts to wear a leek. St. David, who lived in the 5th and 6th centuries, was Archbishop of Caerleon, and has since become the Patron Saint of Wales. Memory of him has traditionally held a place of high reverence in England as well.

There are many stories and legends that have grown up about St. David, including one early Welsh manuscript which claims to show him being the eighteenth in lineal descent from the Virgin Mary. It is also rumoured that, when he died in 544, he was 140 years old. Apparently, St. David's life was a model for all. He founded a convent in the Vale of Rhos, and was made Primate of Wales in 519. He was buried in the Cathedral at Menevia, now known as St. David's, close to the westernmost tip of Wales in Dyfed.

There are various stories accounting for the wearing of a leek on St. David's Day. One is that it commemorates a critical battle that the Britons won over the Saxons, in which the former, by order of St. David, wore a leek in their hats as their colours. Another is supported by Shakespeare in *Henry V*, in which Fluellin tells the king that the custom originated at the battle of Cressy, where Welshmen under Henry V's great uncle, Edward the Black Prince of Wales, fought bravely in a field where leeks were growing. A third version, more commonly ascribed to, is that leeks were one of the few vegetables available during these lean months and it was customary for farmers to join together and help less fortunate neighbours in their ploughing if the latter had not been able to accomplish it by St. David's Day. The housewives would come along for these communal ploughings, and leeks often made up a large part of the pot-luck meals they prepared.

March 17 is **St. Patrick's Day**. It is a day of national celebration in Ireland and, to a lesser degree, is also honoured in England. Although St. Patrick's birthplace is unknown, England, Scotland,

Wales, Ireland and France have all laid claim to it. He was born about 372 and, at the age of sixteen was kidnapped by pirates and sold into slavery in Ireland. After seven years, he escaped, and was successively ordained a deacon, priest and then Bishop on the Continent, before being sent back to Ireland with Pope Celestine's authority to convert the heathen natives. It was the same Pope who gave him the name Patricius when making him a Bishop, Patrick's original name having been Maenwyn. He managed to woo the Irish away from the older Druidical beliefs, and legend has it he used the shamrock, or three-leafed clover, to point out to them that the Father, Son and Holy Ghost were just as feasible as three leaves growing from a single stalk. Others claim that the number three was already a magical one to the Druids, who considered the mistletoe sacred - since its berries and leaves grew in groups of three -, and whom had long used clover for medicinal purposes. Whatever the real reason, followers of St. Patrick sport a shamrock in his memory on this day.

In the Middle Ages, religious – or mystery – plays were used as a popular method of communicating Biblical history to the masses. In addition to it being St. Patrick's Day, March 17 was also celebrated in medieval England as the day when Noah was supposed to have entered the ark. **Mystery plays** on this theme were performed, and the wits of the day took humorous liberties with Noah's wife, who was exaggerated into an archetypal middle-ages shrew. In one of the earliest of these plays available, she berates Noah for his credulity when he tells her of the coming flood, claiming that he is a habitual bearer of bad news. They come to blows and grapple on the stage until he manages to escape, so he can work on the ark. Later in the play, she refuses to enter the finished ark ...until forced to by the threatening impending danger of the rising flood. No sooner is she on the ark than she starts nagging him, and they end up fighting again. Their three sons, meanwhile, stand by and shake their heads over the family conflicts.

In another version, there is a scene in a tavern, and Noah's wife refuses to enter the ark unless she can bring her gossips along, telling him he can find another wife if he doesn't like her terms. In the Canterbury Tales, Chaucer suggests through his character Nicholas that Noah might have preferred his wife to have had a ship of her own.

The next fixed feast day is March 25, which honours the annunciation of the Blessed Virgin Mary, commemorating her message from the Archangel Gabriel that the Word was become flesh; the timing intended to be consistent with the setting of Christ's birthday on December 25, nine months later. It has traditionally been known in England as **Lady Day**. It used to be considered as the first day of the new year and, falling as it does almost precisely on the vernal equinox, was originally one of the four quarter days in the old agricultural calendar. It subsequently became, for legal purposes, one of the four days in the year when rent payments became due. In some parts of England, tenancies may still be timed to begin and end on Lady Day.

One of England's oldest charities, the **Tichborne Dole**, is performed each year in Hampshire. Tradition has it that, in the 12th century, a Lady Mabella was on her deathbed and begged her husband, Lord Tichborne, to provide her with the means of leaving a bequest that those in want might receive a gift of bread annually on the feast of the Annunciation. He, being a mean sort, told her that she would be welcome to use the proceeds from as much land as she could walk around, so long as a brand he held was still burning. The good lady was so weak she had to be carried by her attendants in a cot out to the fields. She was also too sickly to walk, and had to resort to crawling around the field, while her husband stood by holding the burning brand. She managed, perhaps miraculously, to make it around twenty-three acres, a field which, until recent times, has still been called the *Crawl*. Before she died, she warned her husband that if his word wasn't kept, and the dole not distributed on Lady Day, the family fortunes would fail and their name die out. According to the legend, she added that the signs would be a generation of seven sons, the next generation having seven daughters, and the collapse of the family mansion. The dole was strictly observed until 1796, when the local gentry complained at the hordes of idlers and beggars who would congregate in that vicinity on March 25.

A recent incumbent family head, Sir Henry Tichborne, directed the revenues from the Crawl to the Church. Coincidentally, part of his house collapsed in 1803, and he had seven sons, the eldest of which had seven daughters. Sir Henry's third son re-instated the dole, and it has continued ever since. There was a difficult year in 1948, when bread rationing was in effect in England, and the Ministry of Food hesitated about permitting the dole to be carried out. However, the public outcry from all over England was so strong that they relented. Today, the dole is given in flour, which is made from wheat grown in the *Crawl*. The ceremony includes an open-air Catholic service with a blessing of the flour, and prayers are said for Lady Mabella.

Mid-Lent, or **Mothering Sunday**, is a moveable feast occurring on the fourth Sunday in Lent, which usually falls in the latter half of March. There are conflicting stories of its origin, but the most likely one is that it was a day set aside by faithful pre-Reformation parishioners for attending services at the Mother Church, or Cathedral, of their parish or diocese. After the Reformation, it became one of the few holidays permitted by employers throughout rural England, and young domestics and farm labourers would use the day to visit their families. Usually, they would bring their mothers a cake and present her with a bunch of wildflowers, which they had gathered on their way home. The day was seen as a welcome respite from the abstention of Lent, and different regions of England had varying specialities for the celebration, including furmenty, or grain boiled in sweetened and spiced milk in the Midlands and South, and carlings, a pancake made of peas fried in butter in the northern parts of the country.

In other locations in the northern counties and Scotland, the carlings were traditionally enjoyed a week later on Passion Sunday, which became known as Care, or Carling, Sunday. The two foods most commonly associated with Mothering Sunday, however, are simnel cakes and Mothering
Sunday wafers.

Simnel Cakes

Herrick alludes to the cake in these verses from
Hesperides, written in 1648:

"I'll to thee a simnel bring,
'Gainst thou go a-mothering;
So that, when she blesses
thee,
Half that blessing thou'lt give me."

Simnel comes from the Latin word *simila*, and this was the whitest and finest flour available in the early middle ages. In those times, it appeared only in larders of the most affluent. Later on, it came to be associated with the fine flours reserved for making cakes to be consumed on special occasions. In some of the western counties, including Shropshire and Herefordshire, the crust is baked, after being brushed with egg, from dough made with this fine flour, coloured deep yellow with saffron. The cake's interior is formed of a rich plum-cake, which has been boiled.

Mothering Sunday practices began to decline around 1900, but had a resurgence of popularity later, attributable principally to its promotion as a more commercialised Mother's Day by card and gift shops, but also partially to its popularity with American servicemen, who wished to honour their English foster-mothers when they were garrisoned in England for two or three years during the Second World War. The English Mothering Sunday has completely different origins from the very popular American Mother's Day, which began to be promoted by Miss Anna Jarvis, of Philadelphia, whose mother had recently died. It soon gained widespread regional following and, after its adherents had lobbied Congress, it was established in 1914 that Mother's Day would be observed nationally on the second Sunday in May.

In addition to ploughing, the farmer proceeds to sow barley and oats if March's dry weather continues, although the sowing process throughout the country can be observed well into April. The value of a dry March for seeding is expressed in different age-old proverbs, such as:

"A bushel of March dust is worth a king's ransom."

And

"A dry March never begs its bread."

The cottage gardens bustle with the activities of pruning, spading and planting of flowers and kitchen gardens. Ducks and geese begin laying and sitting, and bees are seen out of their hives for the first time around the middle of March. Many familiar birds return after their long winter holiday in the south. Some birds, such as the redwing thrush and woodcock, which spend their winter in England, begin disappearing from our landscape returning to their more northerly nesting grounds in Sweden and Norway. Most of the new year's lambs are weaned in March, and allowed the freedom of the pasture as soon as the weather permits. They are one of the most endearing features of the English countryside, gambolling and racing with each other around the fields, eager to explore the fresh new world about them, but eager, too, to return to their mother when the ewe summons them with a familiar bleat.

APRIL

When April blows its horn,
'Tis good for hay and corn.

Etymologically, April has a variety of origins to choose from. Ovid claims the source for *Aprilis* was *Aphrodite*, the Greek name for Venus. Another early writer, Macrobius, agreed that this was probable as the ancients' method of tempering the fiery origins of the preceding month's namesake with the gentler qualities of their goddess of beauty and love. Others averred the name came from the Latin verb *aperire*, to open, and reflected the seasonal unfolding of leaves and buds, as well as the fertile earth's willingness to open itself once again to the new year's seeds. If this latter claim is correct, April would stand out as the only month in our calendar which possesses a name reflecting the natural conditions of the weather and seasons.

The Saxon name for this month was *Oster-monat.* *Ost* in Anglo-Saxon meant East, and the name is thought to derive from the easterly winds which prevail during this month.

Throughout recorded history April has had a chequered history in regard to its number of days and positioning in the year. In the early Alban calendar, which had ten irregular months, April was the first month, and had 36 days. In the subsequent Romulus calendar, it took second place and had 30 days. Following Numa Pompilius's revision of the calendar, April was given fourth place in the year, but had only 29 days. The 30 days the month now has is due to Julius Caesar's later reformation.

April's weather is notable for its changeableness, bringing us some of the finest days of the year intermixed with cold, rainy days which, in contrast to the warm sunshine, remind us of the worst days of winter.

The elm, ash and oak begin to look half-dressed in this month, with their budding leaves, and the fields and meadows acquire a fresh, green and jewelled sheen. Apple, peach, cherry, plum and other fruit trees burst into colourful blossoms, stirring the newly awakened bee from his long winter's hibernation.

Popular birds are another distinguishing characteristic of the month. The returning swallow family is a welcome herald of the coming summer. The chimney swallow and house make their nests under eaves and windows, while the arriving swift burrows under roof tiles. Pairing, nest-building and brooding are major preoccupations of April. The birds' industry gives remarkable illustrations of carpentry, weaving and joinery; reminders of duty just when our hearts long most to be out enjoying an unproductive rural walk, or the year's first outdoor lunch at a rustic country pub. Soon after the swallow's return the nightingale is heard again. This enchanting bird sings both night and day, but can be discerned more obviously at night when the other noisy neighbours, like the thrush, redbreast and blackbird, are asleep. As with the birds, insects make their presence known once more. The cricket resumes its interminable and monotonous call along the riverbanks and dragonflies emerge from the water. The warmth draws fish out in search of food. If they are not wary, they soon become someone else's meal, for the angler is another of April's characters, nurturing Izaak Walton's words as he idles by a stream or river:

> Oh the gallant fisher's life,
> It is the best of any;
> 'Tis full of pleasure, void of strife,
> And 'tis beloved by many...

Just as nature breathes new life into the earth and wildlife, so are the sentiments of spring awakened in the young and old. The month opens on a note of levity with **All Fools' Day** on April first. It has traditionally been a popular day for playing random pranks on family and friends.

Exacting qualities are demanded of the accomplished practitioner. They must have an inventive turn of mind to work out a supposed fact or story which is barely plausible and best suited to the victim nearest to hand. They must be able to pass this off as the truth, all the while maintaining a perfectly straight face. Only when the victim falls for the carefully prepared bait is the imposture revealed with the charge "April Fool!" There are a variety of traditional April Fool's jokes which are marched out year after year, such as telling someone that there is a spider somewhere on their person, or that their shoelaces are untied. Before shoelaces became popular, the same prank was played with buckles.

The fool's errand has also been perennially popular, and includes such favourites as sending a naive acquaintance to a shop to purchase *A History of Eve's Grandmother*, or a quantity of pigeon's milk or elbow grease.
Chambers quotes a less savoury example of a woman who stole a watch on the first of April and, when caught tried to pass it off as an April Fool's joke. The judge called her the April Fool and gave her a sentence lasting until the next first of April.

In the Border counties and Scotland, the day is known as Gowkie Day, a gowk being a cuckoo. A likely victim is chosen and sent on a fool's errand, with a message telling its recipient to "Hunt the gowk another mile," and the fool is sent on a second gowk's errand with a new similar message, and so on.

All Fool's Day is, in fact, only a half-day celebration. For some unknown reason, the practical joking traditionally ended at noon. After that, if any further deceptions were attempted, the perpetrator would become the fool, when his victim recited a stock formula, such as:

Twelve o'clock is past and gone
And you're a fool for making me one.

or,

April Fool's gone and past
You're the biggest fool at last.

April Fool's sport played by children on a passerby

The origins of All Fool's Day are unknown, although several theories have been hazarded by historians. *Poor Robin's Almanac* for 1750 quoted the verse:

> The first of April, some do say,
> Is set apart for All Fools' Day,
> But why the people call it so,
> Nor I nor they themselves do know.

Although the Catholic Church has ties to the Feast of the Ass and the earlier Festival of the Fools, both these celebrations occurred on other dates.

The All Fools' Day practices seem to have as their object an increase in popular esteem for the wit at the expense of his poor dupe, who is made the laughing-stock of any bystanders. Perhaps the custom once had another object. The proximity of the first of April to New Year, Old Style, on March 25, seems to imply that humbling experiences incurred early in the year would benefit all concerned.

The character of the Fool appears also in various Mystery Plays, as well as with some examples of Morris Dancers.

Just as early Kings had their wise jesters, there seems to be an ancient and inextricable intermingling of the ideas of Wisdom and Folly.

That the custom is extremely old has some support in the fact that very similar 'April Fool's jokes' are played by Hindus of all ranks and ages during their festival of *Holi*, an ancient celebration ending March 31, which honours the beginning of spring.

Although our everyday lives present us with many occasions throughout the year when we would dearly love to call others fools, the tradition of April the first seems to have survived because we are given licence to do so with impunity on that one-half day each year.

April usually has the generous share of festivities associated with that most important of moveable feasts, Easter. First on the list is **Palm Sunday**, the last of Lent, and then Holy Week, including Maundy Thursday, Good Friday and Easter Sunday, followed by Hocktide a week later.

Palm Sunday celebrates Jesus's triumphal entry into Jerusalem when the people
'took branches of palm trees and went forth to meet him, and cried, Hosanna...' and strew their branches along his route. In Roman times it was customary to litter a hero's path with palm branches. Elaborate ceremony surrounds the annual Palm Sunday rituals in Rome and, throughout the Roman Catholic world the priest will bless the palm leaves, after which they are carried by the people in a procession in memory of that first Palm Sunday.

In pre-Reformation England similar practices were followed. At some churches, the events of the entry to Jerusalem were re-enacted during the procession. A wooden model of an ass on wheels, upon which was mounted the figure of Jesus, would be drawn along behind priests chanting psalms. The parishioners would throw their branches on the wooden figure or lay them down in its path. As soon as it had been drawn over the leaves, they would gather them up again to keep until the next year as talismans against the effects of inclement weather. Palm Sunday practices remained part of the official rites of the Church of England until the reign of Edward VI (1547-1553). Subsequently, the processions fell into disfavour and were viewed by some of our more puritanical ancestors as idolatrous and empty pageantry. However, the innocent practice of going 'a-palming' just before Palm Sunday continued to be observed in rural England. Instead of palm leaves, though, other available leaves are used, usually the sallow willow with its velvety yellow buds, but

Palm Sunday

sometimes the box or yew. These were gathered in the fields and used to decorate homes or churches, as well as to be sported in buttonholes and hats.

The derivation of the name **Passion Week**, which succeeds Palm Sunday and culminates in Easter, comes from the original meaning of that word, suffering, and commemorates the crucifixion on Golgotha.

Maundy Thursday, during this week, has become characterised by acts of humility and charity. Ecclesiastics, monarchs and nobles, especially during medieval times, have marked the occasion by washing the feet of the poor and distributing clothes, money or baskets of food, imitating the actions of Jesus on that first Maundy Thursday. The baskets in which the food was given were known as *maunds* and it is thought that the day's name derives from this. Others theorize the origin is from the word mandatum referring to Christ's mandate at the Last Supper, "A new commandment I give unto you, that ye love one another." English monarchs washed the feet of the poor as part of their Royal Maundy duties from as early as King John in 1212. The practice continued up until James II's time, after which the chore was delegated to the Lord High Almoner. Today the Royal Maundy includes a distribution of money by the Monarch or the Lord High Almoner, the Archbishop of Canterbury, during the Maundy Thursday service.

Good Friday follows and honours the day on which Jesus was crucified. The epithet 'Good' is thought to come from the word 'God', and recalls the completion of Christ's good, or 'Godly', work which led to man's redemption. The Saxons also knew it as Long Friday, possibly due to the lengthy services and fasts which were observed on this day. Together, the combination of Good Friday and Easter, which we move through year after year, present us with that enigmatic paradox upon which the Christian religion is founded: seeming death and resurrection. Dramas involving the same, or a similar subtle riddle were re-enacted in much older religions in Egypt, and in the even more ancient worship of the Mystery of the Seed. Good Friday has, since earliest Christianity, honoured the first half of this bi-fold secret by playing night to Easter's day.

It was the rural English practice to perform only unavoidable chores on this day, as well as to attend an unusually solemn church service. In a few locations no other work was consider proper, but in many of the countries it became traditional to use the rest of the day for sowing. Favourites for Good Friday planting were potatoes and parsley. Presumably, the combined propinquity and certainty of Easter were linked to spring's regeneration of the earth and plant life. The holiness of the day was thought to guarantee an abundant yield. Even in urban England the esteem in which Good Friday was held can be reckoned by the fact that not much more than a hundred years ago it was one of only two days in the year – the other being Christmas - during which all commerce ceased.

In spite of the solemnity of the occasion, Good Friday has its lighter and more enjoyable conventions. One of the oldest and most popular traditions is that of eating **hot cross buns** early in the morning. Although they are now provided by supermarkets and bakeries, it used to be common in towns to awaken to vendors in the streets, with their baskets tucked under their arms, singing:

> Hot cross buns!
> Hot corss buns!
> One a penny, two a penny,
> Hot cross buns!
> If you have no daughters,
> Give them to your sons:
> But if you have none of these merry little elves
> Then you may keep them all to yourselves!

The street vendor's basket would be covered by a white cloth and flannel, for it was essential the product be 'piping hot'. The buns are traditionally regularly shaped, but have their sweet surface marked with the sign of the cross. The taste, though, is quite different from a normal bun in that the dough usually contains currants and a flavouring of allspice. When heated, the pervading aroma of the allspice – a seeming combination of cinnamon, nutmeg and cloves – brings to many minds the reminder of holidays and of festive baked goods, but especially of these buns which are eaten on Good Friday.

The Christian use of the buns with a cross on them dates from the time of Constantine in the fourth century. However, many pre-Christian pagans offered up sacrificial cakes to their gods, notably the Queen of Heaven, a practice condemned by the prophet Jeremiah. In ancient Greece and Egypt the cross appearing on these sacred cakes was intended to represent the horns of the sacrificial ox. Later, similar smallish loaves marked with crossed lines were discovered in bakeries in Herculaneum and Pompeii, both of which cities were destroyed when Mount Vesuvius erupted in 79 A.D. It is thought the purpose of the lines on these was not Christian in origin, but simply as a method which facilitated the breaking of the bread. For English parishioners, hot cross buns developed into something of a lay sacrament, approaching in quality the merits of consecrated bread itself, especially if they were baked on Good Friday. In rural homes not so long ago, one or more of these would be hung in the kitchen for luck, until the next anniversary of the day rolled around. It was thought that the grated powder of these buns would act as a cure for many ailments, particularly indigestion and diarrhoea.

Many widely separated communities enjoyed Good Friday fairs and picnics, and in the south east counties of Surrey, Sussex and Cambridgeshire the day also went by the name of **Marble Day** or **Long Rope Day**, its festive air being increased through the local enthusiasm for games of marbles or an annual custom of skipping. The skipping is thought to have stemmed from the idea of newly planted seeds springing up through the earth. It would go on for hours with breaks for picnic-styled snacks. Large groups from individual villages would participate and long ropes would be used, so that several could jump at the same time.

The marble season, begun on Ash Wednesday, followed the course of Lent, and wound up with serious championship matches which had to terminate at the stroke of noon on Good Friday. Marbles could be confiscated if you were caught playing with them after mid-day. Such matches date from the sixteenth century. The most famous continuation until recently has been at Tinsley Green near Crawley, West Sussex. The solemnity with which the game is played is underlined by the story of an Elizabethan girl who let a game of marbles decide which of her suitors she would marry.

At Tinsley Green the game has strict rules. There are six competitors to a match, and forty-nine marbles are placed in a circle with a six-foot diameter. Each of the competitors shoots his *tolley*, or marble, and tries to knock as many marbles out as possible. Players must shoot their marble without moving their hand, using the force of the thumb alone. If no marbles are hit out and a player's *tolley* remains in the ring, it must be left there, and that competitor waits until his next turn to try again. If his *tolley* stays in the ring, but he manages to knock any other marble out, he may have another go. The winning team is the first to knock 25 marbles out of the circle.

Many ecclesiastics rate **Easter** as the most important religious celebration of the year, followed closely by Christmas and Whit Sunday. Unlike the festival of Christmas, there is little doubt that Easter has been celebrated continuously since the Resurrection of Christ, which is popularly thought to have occurred in 33 A.D. At first the apostles kept the joyous anniversary, and then their early followers perpetuated the commemoration.

The Sage of Jarrow, the Venerable Bede (*c.* 673-735), agreed with the general consensus that Easter's name comes from Eostre, the Saxon goddess of spring. Her festival was reverently observed by the Saxons each spring long before the first waves of Christian missionaries set foot in England. Once Christianized, the Saxon folk readily took to the Easter customs which, like their spring rites, honoured the resurrection of life. They re-enacted the Biblical story in their churches, having their women parishioners discover the empty tomb which had been set beside the altar. Later Paschal dramas and special songs were added to further embroider the solemn occasion.

In Medieval England, many churches symbolically remembered the drama of the crucifixion by extinguishing all fires and lights before beginning the Midnight Mass in total darkness. Then, during the service, the great Paschal candle was lit with flint and steel to represent the great light that came into men's lives with the Resurrection. Other candles were lit from this first one until, at last, in the interior of the church, the night of Passion was transformed into the radiant dawn of Easter. In English homes of that time a new, or 'need' fire was struck in the grates on an Easter morning. Parishioners of Orthodox Churches remember the day's significance by greeting each other with the joyous news, "Christ is risen!" - to which the response is "He is risen indeed!"

Just as Mark tells us how Mary "came into the sepulchre at the rising of the sun", so has it been traditional for the devout to awaken early on Easter to watch that same sun rise in the heavens. In the southern counties it was a common belief that, from a hilltop at dawn on this day, a lucky few would be able to see the sun dance on the horizon or, even better, to descry the shape of the Paschal Lamb against the burning disc.

Since time immemorial eggs have been used to represent the idea of new life, and it was only natural they would be adopted as an important symbol denoting the Resurrection. In many places the **Easter Egg** is known as the 'Pace Egg' from the word Paschal. Pope Pius V assigned a prayer to English churches for use in blessing the Paschal Eggs: "Bless, O Lord, we beseech Thee, this Thy creature of eggs, that it may become a wholesome sustenance to Thy faithful servants, eating in thankfulness to Thee, on account of the Resurrection." Eggs accordingly formed an important part of Easter's fare, and were eagerly looked forward to, more so as they had traditionally been banned from the table during Lent. Lamb was also favoured, as it was thought to have been served at the Last Supper. Tansy cakes or puddings were another food traditionally enjoyed on Easter. They were heavily flavoured with the herb tansy and meant to be eaten with meat, rather than as a dessert. The origin of the tansy cake is believed to be with the bitter herbs used by the Jews in dishes prepared for Passover.

Many of Easter's folk customs have developed around the egg: egg-shackling, egg-rolling, pace-egging and the children's favourite, the morning hunt in the garden for eggs hidden by the Easter Hare. Unlike Christmas, for which lengthy preparations begin at Advent, Easter decorations are usually made up only just before the day itself. The most universal of these is the decorated Easter Egg, brightly dyed, hand-painted or, in earlier days, with a drawing etched on a previously dyed egg.

Egg-shackling was a favourite game among schoolboys. Each would hold his treasured hard-boiled egg in his hand and use it to hit another lad's egg. The winner was the one whose egg remained intact, and the broken egg became his spoils. One of the professed secrets of this sport lies in the belief that the sooner an egg is boiled after it is laid, the harder it becomes.

 In Yorkshire, Lancashire and further northern counties, **egg-rolling** became a tradition. The natives of different communities would get together at a grassy hill and roll coloured hard-boiled Easter Eggs down them. At some locations, the winner was the one whose egg went through a goal set at the bottom of the hill, or the one whose egg was last to break. Usually, though the custom was enjoyed more in a non-competitive fashion, and the owners ate their broken eggs after they'd had the fun of colouring and rolling them. The custom is thought to have originated from the association of the rolling away of the stone in front of Christ's tomb.

Pace-Egging is a practice which still survives in northern parts of England, albeit usually in a modified form. Originally young men and boys would dress up as mummers in various costumes, with ribbons and streamers attached to their clothes, and perform a Pace-Egg play in the surrounding towns. In return they would expect to be given eggs or other gifts. More recently, the play is generally omitted, and the custom has been taken over by children who enjoy making the rounds and begging gifts from their neighbours. In Howitt's *Pictorial Calendar of the Seasons* (1854) children in Chesire are reported to have gone around asking for "an egg, bacon and cheese or an apple, or any good thing to make us merry ...and I pray you, good dame, an Easter egg." Young men in most locations, however, would be sure to request that the gift of eggs be accompanied by some strong beer.

The hare is supposed to have been a sacred animal to the pagan goddess Eostre, as well as to the spring goddesses of other lands. The connection of spring with this furry beast may well have its origins in the amusing activities of the mad March hare in our own countryside. We have inherited the widespread Continental folklore that the hare somewhat magically provides the **Easter Eggs** which children so love to **hunt**. Similarly, **hare-pie scrambling** and **hare hunts** formed a part of earlier Easter traditions in numerous villages.

Easter Lifting, or Heaving, used to be widely practiced on Easter Monday and Tuesday. The men would lift women on the Monday, sometimes in a chair decorated for that purpose, and demand a ransom. The roles would be reversed on the Tuesday with the women lifting the men. Money thus collected was usually given to the parish church. Lifting customs are said to be connected with the idea of the Resurrection, but the components of a victim and a ransom suggest origins in pre-Christian spring sacrificial rites.

The Sunday after Easter is called Low Sunday, probably due to its relative unimportance after the joyous outbursts of the week before. However, it used to be followed by a **Hocktide** celebration on the Monday and Tuesday. The festivities consisted of enjoyable sports and games and, in the Middle Ages, a Hock Play re-enacting the defeat of the Danes by Ethelred in 1002. Although the origins of the word 'Hock' are uncertain, the accepted purpose became the raising of funds for pious uses.

Tying in with spring's Resurrection theme, April witnesses our birds brooding over their multicoloured eggs, and the hatching of ducks and geese. The phenomenal cacophony made by birds in the spring is only approached once more when autumn comes around. All of this singing is often ascribed to courtship, but seems more likely to be in part a reflex action prompted by the fine weather. A great deal of rural folklore has attached itself to the **cuckoo**, who returns to our greening countryside sometime in April and whose activities were thought to give us something of a spring and summer calendar:

> In April
> Come she will,
> In flowery May
> She doth sing all day,
> In leafy June
> She doth change her tune
> In bright July
> She doth begin to fly,
> In August
> Go she must.

April 21st was the generally accepted date the cuckoo would first make its appearance in many parts of the country. In the Middle Ages it was thought that the bird had the singular power of predicting how many more years a person would live, if the question were asked when its notes were first heard. The number of times the bird called after the question was put gave the years of life remaining. In northern Europe, it was believed that the cuckoo did not build its own nest as a consequence of being so busy giving prophetic answers to this question. Its peculiarity of leaving its eggs in the nests of other birds has given rise to our English word cuckold. Another popular superstition held that one's principal employment throughout the year would depend upon what one was doing when the cuckoo was first heard. If you were lucky enough to have money in your pocket on this occasion, not always an easy matter for our ancestors after a difficult winter, it was believed that you would not lack for it for the next twelve months. The novelty of hearing the first cuckoo soon wears off, for the bird's name comes from the male's monotonous repetition of that single sound, which prompted Chaucer to urge it "Now, good cuckowe, goe somewhere away."

Just as the cuckoo's arrival is dependent on the natural calendar, so are the farmers unable to rely on the solar calendar used for civic purposes. Weather conditions frequently vary from year to year, and they must look to other natural signs to judge the most appropriate timing of their activities. One example of this is the time fixed for shearing the sheep. If performed before it is warm enough, there is the danger of losing too many of the animals to exposure. Hence this particular chore cannot be fixed to a specific day each year. An early method of determining the proper time for shearing was based on the flowering of the elder tree, as usually a safer degree of warmth from the advancing season was necessary before this would occur.

In contradistinction to this requirement for a natural calendar, a great variety of fixed dates are believed to be efficacious for ploughing, sowing and reaping, their variety usually depending on the latitude in which the sayings were popularized. April 23rd, **St. George's Day**, is one of these. A rural expression, "St. George to borrow" arose as it was presumed that by this day a farmer would be able to make a reasonable estimate of how much produce his land would yield for the year. This would permit him to borrow money based on the estimated collateral value of his crop projections, an amount which could be independently verified by the lender.

In addition to his part in this rural maxim, St. George holds a prominent niche in legend and history as England's patron saint. The original St. George was thought to have been either a Christian officer in the Roman army who was martyred around the year 300for his faith by Diocletian...or by the rapacious Archbishop of Alexandria, who was in turn killed by vengeful mobs in 303. The famous dragon legend, written up by Voragine in *The Golden Legend* during the thirteenth century, puts St. George in Silene in Libya, where the citizens had to feed two sheep per day to a dragon to keep it at bay. When they ran out of sheep, they had to begin substituting with their children. On the day St. George put in an appearance it was the King's daughter's turn to be devoured. Our saint slew the dragon in return for the citizens' promise to be baptised, and thus was credited with saving the princess's life, along with some fifteen thousand souls. St. George's fame was bolstered during the Crusades, when he was reported to have appeared and fought for Godfrey de Bouillon at Antioch in 1098, and to similarly have heralded a victory against the Saracens for Richard I, Coeur de Lion. He became a patron saint of soldiers, and was associated with chivalry and the famous battle-cries using his name. In 1222 St. George's Day was declared a holiday and, around 1344, Edward III founded the Order of St. George, more popularly known as the Order of the Garter, to honour the bravest of his knights.

St. George

St. George's Day celebrations rose and fell in popularity with alternate monarchs after the Reformation, and were widely neglected by the end of the 1800s, in spite of the fact that the 23rd was also believed to have been both the birth and death dates of Shakespeare. More recently there has been something of a revival of the celebration dotted around the country. The approved badge for the day is the national flower, a red rose, worn in the buttonhole. In some places a pageant is held using the characters of the Saint and his dragon. Many churches can be seen flying the flag of St. George, a simple red cross on a white field, and the gold sovereign still usually depicts St. George slaying the dragon on its reverse side.

St. Mark's Day is the 25th, and a goodly number of superstitions used to be attached to its eve. Among rural villages it was commonly believed that the spirits of those who would die in the following year could be seen entering the parish church between 11pm and 1am. Another practice still prevalent in some counties a century ago was the making of a dumb-cake in complete silence by three unmarried girls. At the stroke of midnight each would eat a portion of the cake and then walk backwards to their beds. If they were destined to marry, they were supposed to be able to see the images of their future husbands following them, or to perceive some other propitious omen. Alternatively, a smock would be hung up by the fire and a lucky maiden who watched it would wait for the likeness of her future husband to come and turn the garment.

> On St. Mark's eve, at twelve o'clock,
> The fair maid will watch her smock,
> To find her husband in the dark,
> By praying unto good St. Mark.

Another method was divination using nuts. A row of them, one from each maiden, would be planted among the hot embers of the hearth, and the name of each maiden's loved one would be breathed by her. If the love was to be successful, it was believed the nut she had placed in the row would jump away from the fire ...but that otherwise the embers would consume it.

St. Mark's Eve

As April draws to a close, we eagerly look forward to the prospect of summer. Cowslips begin to dot the pastures and golden daffodils can be seen shaking their heads in the April winds. A deep sigh of relief is heaved as we see the last of the winter's store of carrots and potatoes disappear from the table, and some fresh foods from the garden become available; herbs for salads and soups, asparagus, radishes and rhubarb. Beetroot, broccoli and leeks can be relied on to vary the family's vegetable fare.

In some districts April carollers would make the rounds of their neighbourhoods in the latter half of the month to herald summer's coming with May Singing. The singers, known as 'Mayers', were usually accompanied by a flute or clarinet. The standard rule was that the May songs *had* to be sung before the first day of the month. This was in the apparent belief they would help chase away the cold winter.

MAY

Mist in May, heat in June,
Makes the harvest come right soon.

The ancient Alban calendar gave May twenty-two days and placed it as the second month of the year. In the subsequent Romulus calendar, it took third place and had thirty-one days. Later, Numus Pompilius gave it its present position, fifth, but removed one day. Julius Caesar finally returned its thirty-first day, and May has remained unchanged since that time.

Our name for the month is thought to have come from the Latin _Maius_ or _Majus_ (from _Majores_) but, as in other months, the reasons for that nomenclature have been variously disputed. The most likely basis is that it was named in honour of the senate provided for by the original constitution of Rome. Romulus had split the populace into two classes; the elders, or _Majores_, who governed by their counsels, and the juniors, or _Juniores_, who maintained the republic by their arms. May was named for the former while June honoured the latter.

It is appropriate that, just as this month lionises the Roman senate, our Saxon fathers held their own parliament in May. In this _folkmote_, or convention, the freemen, aldermen, thanes and bishops would gather, and the laymen among them would swear to defend the laws of the realm and each other before proceeding to more prosaic business. However, they called the month _Tri-milki_, giving thanks to the new spring growth, which allegedly now allowed them to milk their cows three times a day. Right up until the change in the calendar in 1752, May Day, Old Style, was still considered the appropriate time to turn the cattle back out to pasture. A vast improvement in the milk from the fresh grass was enjoyed over that which had come from the increasingly poorer winter fodder. With the fresh milk the cheese-making industry would begin anew, especially in those counties renowned for their distinctive traditional cheeses.

As eager as we are for summer, May is still decidedly a spring month, and strong easterly winds continue to be felt. The early part of the month can be quite cool, especially since the loss of eleven days with the change to the Gregorian calendar. To this coolness is ascribed the rural admonition

> Change not a clout
> Til May be out.

meaning that, for the prudent, it was still too early to don lighter summer clothing. The grass is now tall enough for children to play hide and seek in, and the hedgerows blossom with hawthorn, commonly known as the Maybud. Maiden would wash their faces with dew shaken from the May, as it was considered something of an elixir for the complexion. Buttercups raise their heads above the grass and cover the meadows with a golden hue made all the brighter for their contrast with the green. It used to be thought that the buttercup gave the yellow colour to butter until it was discovered that cows do not like the plant's acrid taste. The wood-sorrel also blooms at this time. It was the original Irish shamrock before that honour passed to the clover plant. The sweet woodruff, with a smell like new hay, would be gathered to impart a fresh scent to the wardrobe.

In the continuing march of the seasons, May gives us a generous share of natural changes, and it seems that in each day during it we can delight in a new sight or sound. The air is filled with the noise of birds; the lark, cuckoo, thrush, blackbird and nightingale. The latter so penetrate the clear night air with its lovely music that Izaak Walton declared, "Lord, what music hast Thou provided for the saints in heaven, when Thou affordest bad men such music on earth!" In the churchyard yews rooks are heard cawing around their ancestral homes. There is an industrious buzzing from bees, and swarms begin leaving their old hives to start new colonies, following the whims of their Amazonian queen. Other new insects include the horse-fly, the may-chaffer and an astonishing variety of multi-coloured butterflies which flitter in the air and feed on flowers through their long proboscises. After the sun sets the glow work can be discerned shining in the darkness. It is the wingless female which glows; the male of this species having been given wings, perhaps to console it for not being luminous.

The trees fill out with leaves, and soon we have difficulty remembering what the wintry scene was like without them. The month also brings flowers to many trees and shrubs; the oak, beech, maple, mountain ash, sycamore and laburnum. Birds begin to hatch and rear their young. The female has been patiently sitting while the male is usually nearby singing to her. Schoolboys have a new excuse to dawdle on their way to and from the classroom as they hunt out fresh varieties of nests and eggs, while the dedicated angler is observed strolling to his favourite river or stream through the early morning mist.

With all these welcome natural changes, May has, since the earliest times, been set aside as a month for rejoicing and celebration. It begins with **May Day** on the first, which used to be known as the Celtic ***Beltane***, a quarter day in their pastoral calendar on which lambs could safely be let out into the fields. *Bel* was their god representing the summer sun, who had defeated his rival suitor, *Bran*, the winter sun, for the attentions of the Mother Goddess. Happily, whoever was defeated could be resurrected, so the battle could be renewed as the cycle of the seasons progressed. *Tan* in Celtic means fire, and the Druids would light great fires on the fields and cairns to honour their solar hero and to purify the earth for the new season's grazing. Cattle would be driven between these fires in the belief it would protect them from pestilence. At some locations, notably on the Isle of Man, horns and drums would sound through the night to frighten away evil spirits, adding an ominous tumult to the astonishing sight *Bel's* fires made. The Celts assigned the primrose and the marsh marigold to be *Beltane's* herbs, and these were kept against witchcraft. With new herbs available from the woods and gardens, the old dried ones kept for the winter were ceremoniously burnt on the first day of this month.

In some isolated parts of England, where the Celtic stock was least diluted, some of the ancient May Day traditions continued up until fairly recent times. There is a legend that at Holne, near Dartmoor, **ramroasting** was a practice on May 1st. After it was roasted the pieces were distributed to the attending crowds. Another custom for the day was a visit to a Celtic standing stone, in the belief it would cure certain illnesses.

May Day and the few days around it were widely celebrated by the Romans as their **festival of Floralia**, honouring their goddess of flowers, Flora. The beginning of the celebration was heralded with trumpets and floral processions, but it is thought that they ended, like other Roman feasts, in debauchery and intoxication. Similar May Day processions, accompanied by boys decked out in flowers and greenery blowing on cow horns, would march around towns like King's Lynn in Norfolk and Horncastle in Lincolnshire where Roman remains have been discovered.

Just as for the Romans, flowers have played a prominent part in our May 1 customs. **"Going a-Maying"**, or **"Bringing home the May"**, was very popular up until the sixteenth century. Even nobility participated. Chaucer describes May Day in his *Court of Love* with the words,

> And furth goth all the Court, both most and lest,
> To feche the floures fresh, and braunch and blome;
> And namly, hawthorn brought both page and grome,
> With fresch garlandes, partie blewe and whyte ...
> Eke eche, at other threw the floures bright,

People would rise before dawn to gather flowers and hawthorn branches in a spirit of revelry and, accompanied by music, bring them home at sunrise. Doors and windows would be festooned with these happy emblems announcing summer.

May Garlands, made of flowers and greens, would be paraded in many villages. These became so numerous that the day was often called Garland Day. As with Hot Cross Buns, garlands were hawked on the streets by women vendors early in the morning. With the loss of eleven days at the adjustment to the calendar, there has been a significant change in the floral composition of May garlands since the days of Shakespeare and Herrick. Perhaps partly for this reason Garland Day is still observed on May Day, Old Style, at Abbotsbury, Dorset. However the hawthorn and wild rose are usually not in bloom by May 1st, so present day garlands include cowslips, bluebells, lilac and fruit tree blossoms. Various sorts of garlands are made. The easiest is the cowslip ball, knotted in the centre with ribbon or string. Others are made of circles or semi-circles of wire with flower stems looped in spirals around them. A more ingenious one is composed of two or more circles of wire, which are tied together to form the shape of the globe. After the wires are wound with flowers, a cowslip ball is hung in the middle, giving a three-dimensional reminder of the reason for the celebration: the action of the cosmos or, more particularly, the relationship between the sun and the earth and its effects on all blossoming plants. In another similar version, a gold and silver ball are each hung within this floral orrery to represent the sun and moon. After a happy parade through the village, the garland would be hung up over the street, suspended on a rope between two houses, while the festivities continued beneath it. In other places, it was the custom for milkmaids to lead a garlanded cow through the streets and dance round it while a strolling violinist or clarinet-player kept time.

Another long-standing feature of May Day processions has been the **May Queen**, probably as an inherited representation of the Celtic Mother Goddess or the Roman Flora. Usually the part would be played by the prettiest girl in the village, whose reaction to the compliment must certainly have been that expressed in Tennyson's *May Queen*. In some versions she was accompanied by a May

CHILDREN'S MAY-DAY CUSTOMS.

King or a 'Jack in the Green', sometimes known as the 'Green Man', a figure covered in evergreens or flowers, who is thought to represent an early vegetation god, symbolising the rebirth and new growth of the season. In places where the 'Jack in the Green' appeared alone, the procession was known as **"parading the Jack"**. In the Midlands a **Lord and Lady of the May** took the place of a May King and Queen. A number of May Queens are still chosen each year and, in one example reported by Ralph Whitlock in *A Calendar of Country Customs* (1978), three Bedfordshire villages have shared a common May Queen for over 400 years.

In other places the May Queen tradition has been taken over by

children who carry around a doll called their **May Lady**. The doll is
usually nestled in a basket garlanded with flowers, its face hidden by
a piece of lace or a white handkerchief, which is removed to allow
viewing upon the payment of a small ransom in the form of coin or
candy. A version of a May Day carol which children sang as they
paraded their doll or garlands was called "The Mayer's Song", and its
beginning reflects a Christian influence on this ancient pagan
celebration:

> Remember us poor Mayers all,
>   And thus we do begin
> To lead our lives in righteousness,
>   Or else we die in sin.
>
> We have been rambling all this night,
>   And almost all this day,
> And now returned back again,
>   We have brought you a branch of May.
>
> A branch of May we have brought you
>   And at your door it stands,
> It is but a sprout, but it's well budded out
>   By the work of our Lord's hands.

Many people today associate the idea of May Day with the **Maypole**
as a result of the religious controversy which raged around it for
centuries. It is impossible to conceal the fact that its origins are
steeped in the lore of pagan worship and, unlike many other of the
earlier customs, it was never fully Christianised. Chambers, in his
Book of Days, has the following to say about Pope Gregory's sixth
century instructions to Augustine on this topic:

"When Gregory sent Augustine to the conversion of England, the
politic pope gave certain directions for the missionary's guidance.
One referred to the delicate question of how the pagan customs
which already existed among the Anglo-Saxons should be dealt with.
Were they to be entirely abrogated, or were they to be tolerated as far
as was not absolutely incompatible with the religion of the Gospel?
Gregory said that he had thought much on this important subject, and

finally had come to the conclusion that the heathen temples were not to be destroyed, but turned into Christian churches; that the oxen, which used to be killed in sacrifice, should still be killed with rejoicing, but their bodies given to the poor, and that the refreshment booths around the heathen temples should be allowed to remain as places of jollity and amusement for the people on Christian festivals. 'For' he says, 'it is impossible to cut away abruptly from hard and rough minds all their old habits and customs. He who wishes to reach the highest place must rise by steps, and not by jumps.'"

Apparently, although Augustine was successful with many other customs, May Day stubbornly retained its unabashedly pagan spirit as a joyous herald of summer. The Maypole was celebrated by the Goths, too, in Marsburg in northern Germany. They called it the *Irmansul*, meaning 'enormous pillar.' Charlemagne, a staunch Christian, ordered it pulled down in 772. Although the use of Maypoles in England almost certainly predates the Saxon invasion, the first written reference to one seems to be the 'Lostock mepul' mentioned during the

reign of King John (1199-1216). Maypoles grew to be very popular and became permanent fixtures. When the base would rot a new one would replace it in the same spot. In fact, one church in Leadenhall Street is known as St. Andrew Undershaft, because its towers were not as high as the Maypole which stood nearby until 1517, when it was torn down during rioting.

Raising the May-Pole

Maypoles could be made from elm, oak, birch or any straight and sturdy tree. Its trunk would be brought in amidst much revelry and raised in the village green. Usually a flag or a bush was hung from the top, or its upper branches were left on, while the rest would be decorated with spiralling garlands or alternating colours of paint, giving it the appearance of a huge striped barber pole. Once it was raised, all would join in with dancing, feasting and then more dancing into the night, with plentiful refreshment from the alehouse on hand for dancers and musicians alike.

In many locations, the dance involved multi-coloured streamers or ribbons which were hung from the Maypole. These would be drawn out, one to a dancer, to form a large circle about the pole and, after bowing each to his partner, every even member would move clockwise and odd member counter clockwise, braiding in and out among each other in step to the music. As they progressed in their concentric circles, the ribbons, winding round the pole, gradually grew shorter. When the circles became small enough, the watchful band would change the tune and the dancers, about-facing, would return in ever-increasing rounds back to their original positions. A discerning observer can easily draw a parallel between these geometrically balanced configurations and the dramatic and life-giving dance of the planets around their celestial axis. Once drawn, such a conclusion can only lead to wholehearted agreement with the merits of a celebration which annually rejoices at reaching that same May Day position in our solar calendar.

However, not all observers (and probably not all participants) viewed it in this solemn light. The fanatic Philip Stubbes, in his *Anatomie of Abuses* (1583), had the following unkind words with which to describe the celebrants:

"...the chiefest jewel ... is their May-pole, which they bring home with great veneration, as thus. They have twentie or fortie yoke of oxen, every Oxe having sweet nose-gay of flowers placed on the tip of his hornes, and these oxen draw home this May-pole (the stinking Ydol, rather) which is covered all over with floures and hearbs, bound round about with strings from the top to the bottome, and sometime painted with variable colours, with two or three hundred men, women and children following it with great devotion. And thus being reared up with handkercheefs and flags hovering on the top, they straw the ground round about, binde green boughs about it, set up sommer haules, bowers and arbours hard by it; and then fall they to daunce about it, like as the heathen people did at the dedication of the Idols, whereof this is a perfect pattern, or rather the thing itself."

The Maypole fell in and out of fashion in the ensuing years. Shakespeare mentions it in his *A Midsummer's Night Dream* when Hermia unflatteringly describes her rival as a 'painted May-pole.' In spite of this, in Halliwell's later folio edition of Shakespeare's work, a coloured frontispiece depicted the Maypole of Welford, a village very close to Stratford-on-Avon.

King James (1603-1625) supported May games and Maypoles as one of the suitable amusements for Sunday afternoons and holidays in his *Book of Sports*, which was to be read from every pulpit. This sanction, along with permission to enjoy the celebration of other more typically Roman Catholic festivals, was a politic bribe to help convert the peasantry to the new religion. Not long after, though, in 1644, the then powerful Parliament banned festivities on May Day, and on Christmas as well. One of the Ordinances of the Interregnum forbad "prophanation of the Lord's Day by May Pole (a heathenish vanity generally abused to superstition and wickedness)." It went on to add that all extant Maypoles in England and Wales were to be removed by the local churchwardens and constables on penalty of a fine to those officers of five shillings a week until the action was taken.

However, this suppression only served to boost the Maypole to even greater glory after Charles II's restoration. On his first May Day back in power, he had the most famous Maypole in history floated up the Thames and carried in pomp, accompanied by beating drums, from Scotland Yard in Whitehall to Somerset House on the Strand. It was erected by twelve seamen on the island in the street, which is now the site of the little church of St. Mary-le-Strand. It stood 134 feet high and was decorated with crowns, flags and, of course, the Royal Arms, to remind the joyous populace of the glowing future which awaited them under the returned Monarchy. Pepys described the day as "The happiest Mayday that hath been many a year in England" attended by "multitudes of people thronging the streets, with great shouts and acclamations all day long." Although most Maypoles rot at the base within about 15 years, this particular one is reported to have stood for 56 years; so long, in fact, that Drury Lane, which met the Strand at this point, became known as 'May-pole

Alley'. When it finally began to decay, in 1717, it is reported that no other than Sir Isaac Newton arranged for its purchase from the parish, and transported it to an observatory in Essex to support a huge telescope which a French astronomer had presented to the Royal Society.

In the early nineteenth century, the American Washington Irving gave a fresh view and insight into the Maypole in some notes in his *Sketch Book*:

"I shall never forget the delight I felt on first seeing a May-pole. It was on the banks of the Dee, close by the picturesque old bridge that stretches across the river from the quaint little city of Chester ... my fancy adorned it with wreaths of flowers, and peopled the green bank with all the dancing revelry of May-day. The mere sight of the May-pole gave a glow to my feelings and spread a charm over the country for the rest of the day ... and I value every custom that tends to infuse poetical feeling into the common people, and to sweeten and soften the rudeness of rustic manners, without destroying their simplicity."

But Irving was speaking nostalgically, for he went on to lament the great decline in the May Day customs, and suggested that, in spite of contemporaneous attempts to revive them it was unlikely they would ever again achieve their earlier primitive abandon. The decline continued and Chambers, writing of Maypoles in his *Book of Days* (1863), commented "They must now be pretty old people who remember ever seeing one."

Happily, there has been a gradual renewal of many rural customs, and Maypoles now sometimes take a popular place in schoolchildren's May Day. There are, in addition, a number of towns and villages which have a permanent Maypole standing year-round, and whose inhabitants garnish it and keep up the practices each May 1st. Like Irving, one wonders, though, however rustic the village might be, if the present day Maypole festivities attain the simple and joyous exuberance which they occasioned for our medieval ancestors.

In addition to the May Queen, the garlands and the Maypole, further associations which many link with May Day are those of the **Morris Dancers** and Mumming pageants. The word Morris is supposed to have come from 'Moorish'. This derivation is thought to reflect the fact that early Morris Men would blacken their faces, and hence resemble the darker Moors. Morris dances are believed to have originally been pagan fertility rites, and may be an inheritance from those pre-Celtic peoples who inhabited Britain, referred to as 'dark Iberians' in Matthew Arnold's poem *The Scholar Gipsy*.

The Morris Dance

The dance itself, from written descriptions available, has altered little since the late Middle Ages. Morris Men are traditionally made up of a group of six. They are usually decked out in garlanded hats, white or brightly contrasted costumes with bells attached, and clogs on their feet to add rhythmic sounds to their movements. In their hands they wave handkerchiefs, short staves or coloured scarves. The music which accompanies them is often made by a drum, concertina and flute or whistle pipe. Anyone who has observed a Morris dance can easily believe that, if our modern surroundings and accoutrements were replaced by a primeval hut circle, the ceremonial music and movements might well be directed to the attention of a pagan deity in an early prayer for good crops or a plentiful supply of lambs. The steps of each dance impart a sense of formality, as if they have been ritually fixed in ages long past.

For many centuries, Morris Men have been tied to the dances performed around the Maypole, but they are often more recently seen on their own and enjoyed on other occasions. References from around the time of Henry VIII noted differing numbers of dancers including the characters of Robin Hood, Maid Marian, a friar and a musician who played a tabor, a pipe, or both. There has been considerable revival of Morris Dancers. An association of Morris clubs, known as the Morris Ring, was founded with six member groups in the 1930s, and has since grown to more than two hundred associated teams.

Many of the **Mummers Plays** and pageants which were celebrated on May Day evolved from the Celtic idea of the marriage of the earth and the Green Man in the spring. Just as there was an obvious and joyous regeneration evident in their natural surroundings, so did sex add an extra spice to the Celt's May Day; a tradition that was eagerly espoused by later inheritors of their customs. The Celts divided their year into summer and winter, and their festivals of *Beltane* and *Samhain* stood respectively on the dividing line of each of these seasons. As a consequence, these two festival days did not belong to either season, and a relaxation of usual mores was permissible. The villagers would go out at midnight and lose themselves in the darkness of the woods. Some carried stringed instruments or horns, and the sounds of these and of shouts and laughter intermingled with the pairing of couples who had stumbled upon each other in the night gloom of the thickets. Afterwards, when the birds began singing, and the first glimmers of dawn started to peek through the glades, they would deck themselves out in hawthorn and load their arms with flowers and boughs for the embellishment of their homes. Inevitably, children were born of such unions, and their fathers' identities were frequently unknown. There are reports that such offspring latterly assumed the name of Hobson or Robinson, since spring associations came to identify the verdant Robin Hood with the May King and Maid Marian with his queen.

The Calvinist Stubbes, as late as 1583 in his *Anatomie of Abuses*, roundly condemns these orgies:

"For what clipping, what culling, what kissing and bussing, what smooching and slabbering one of another, is not practiced every wher at these dauncings? ... Against May all the yung men and maides, old men and wives, run gadding over night to the woods, groves, hils, and mountains, where they spend all the night in pleasant pastimes: and in the morning they return, bringing with them birch and branches of trees, to deck their assemblies withal. And no mervaile, for there is a great Lord present amongst them, as superintendant and Lord over their pastimes and sportes, namely Sathan prince of hel ... I have heard it creditably reported by men of great gravitie and reputation, that of fortie, threescore, or a hundred maides going to the wood over night, there have scarcely the third part of them returned home againe undefiled."

Such sentiments led to the banning of May Day practices by Cromwell's Parliament. The Puritans saw the May Queen, who was often placed in a bower of greenery set by the Maypole, a a pagan trollop, an object of heathen adoration. Thomas Hall, writing in his *Funebriae Florae* (1660), phrased his rebuke in no uncertain terms: "If Moses were angry when he saw the people dance about the golden calf, well may we be angry to see people dancing the morrice about a post in honour of a whore..."

Many popular May 1st pageants centred around the character of **Robin Hood**, with other players taking the parts of Maid Marian, Little John, Friar Tuck, Will Stukely and an assortment of woodmen with axes archers in green tunics and milkmaids wearing haloes of primroses. Robin Hood, of course, came out the winner in the inevitable archery contest which was an essential component of the celebrations. William Hone's *Every-Day Book* (1826) quotes an account of Henry VIII riding out maying early one morning with Catherine of Aragon from Greenwich to Shooter's Hill,

"...where, as they passed by the way they espied a company of tall yeomen, clothed all in greene hoods, and with bowes and arrowes, to the number of two hundred. One, being their chieftain, was called Robin Hood, who required the King and all his company to stay and see his men shoot ... Moreover this Robin Hood desired the king and queene, with their retinue, to enter the greene wood, where, in arbours made of boughs, and deckt with flowers, they were set and served plentifully with venison and wine, by Robin Hood and his meyny, to their great contentment, and had other pageants and pastimes."

Different May Day dramas and Mumming Plays centre around a beast of sorts. Sometimes the animal is reminiscent of St. George's dragon, but more often is described as a **Hobby Horse**. The most notable examples of these still seen are the ones in Padstow, Cornwall and Minehead, Somerset. The 'Old Oss', as it is locally referred to, is made of a wooden frame, surrounded by a brightly coloured costume which hides the man inside carrying it around. Some Hobby Horses seem to have been used to collect money from door to door, but the money they generate for the towns now comes mostly from the pockets of the hundreds of visitors who flock to see the antics of the Hobby Horses and their accompanying attendants and musicians.

In urban centres, especially London, May 1st used to be recognised as the **chimney-sweeps' holiday**. They would parade the Jack with a drum and fife band and expect to receive half-pennies from bystanders. A further perquisite to their dreary careers on this day included the honour of dancing with the May Queen.

One famous May tradition which has remained virtually unchanged through the centuries takes place on the nearest Saturday to May 8 in Helston, Cornwall. This is the **Furry Dance** whose name may be derived from 'floral' but more likely has its roots in the Cornish *feur* for fair. Many visitors come to Helston each year to watch the celebrations. The populace 'fetch the summer home' at dawn in the form of decorative green boughs. Soon after, at seven am, dancing begins in the streets. Some of the participants wave willow wands as an emblem of the season they are welcoming in. The 'Invitation, or Furry, Dance', heralded by the Mayor, is started at noon, and its female dancers wear their best dresses, while the men are outfitted in morning suits and top hats. This is the chief event of the day, and takes the form of a procession dancing in and out of houses and shops as a method of bringing luck and fertility to their inhabitants. Another feature is the Hal-an-Tow Mummers play and song, replete with such characters as St. George, St. Michael, Robin Hood and a goodly few of the latter's merry men.

Possibly the most expressive May Day pageant was one which took place up until about two hundred years ago on the Isle of Man. Reminiscent of the ancient Celtic *Beltane*, was the staging of an annual **battle between the Queen of Winter and the Queen of May** on the village common. Inevitably the garlanded May Queen was enthroned for the ensuing feast, while the bleak Winter and her forces were banished from the grounds for another year.

After many patient centuries, the Church has managed to get a redeeming foothold into May Day's pagan celebrations. Choirs sing **May Day hymns** at dawn on the 1st at the top of Bargate, Southampton, and the Magdalen Tower in Oxford. The flowers, hawthorn buds and green branches which used to be gathered to garnish the Maypole and homes with also came to be wound around church pillars and to adorn their stained glass windows. More recently, it has been found that some May Day customs are now observed during Whitsuntide, a far more important date to Christians than May 1st, which the Church inauspiciously dedicated to the Apostles Philip and James. Perhaps, then, the plan which St. Augustine and his Pope formed fourteen hundred years ago for the conversion of our heathen ancestors is finally coming to fruition, and soon we may find we have climbed another step on the ladder to the 'highest place' which Gregory spoke of in his sixth century letter.

A great deal of rustic wisdom, probably the result of bitter experience, is summed up in rural admonitions concerning May. One says,

>	A hot May makes a fat churchyard.

While its obverse,

A cold May gives full barns and empty churchyards.

May was, and is, a crucial month, especially when a dreaded famine could be lurking around the corner. There is a long history of blights from wind and insects during this month which can devastate fruit crops. Apple growers in the Southwest counties are especially affected, and apple crops are at a vulnerable stage with all their delicate blossoms exposed. Three days in May are connected with a Devonshire legend concerning this matter. Depending on the version referred to, the period either begins or ends on the 19th and is called after **St. Dunstan** or **St. Frankan**. St. Dunstan died on May 19 in 988. He had been Abbot of Glastonbury and later Archbishop of Canterbury, while St. Frankan appears to have been mythical. The story has the saint employed as a brewer who exchanged his soul to the devil for a promise that a yearly frost would blight the apple crop on these three days in May. This would ensure little or no rival cider production, and a corresponding increase in the volume of his beer sales. The only real basis connecting St. Dunstan with these blights is that the misfortunes often as not occur on or near his feast day, May 19th.

A week later, on the 25th, there is another saying which must have been uttered with a sigh of relief: "Urban brings summer." **St. Urban** was a third century Pope and, during the Middle Ages, this date, his feast day, was thought to herald the start of summer.

With the rural concern over May weather, it was natural that a blessing of crops and a gratitude to the earth and its fruits would be expressed at this time of year. The practice has linked itself to **Rogationtide**, which almost always falls in May. Rogation days are the Monday, Tuesday and Wednesday before Ascension Day, or Holy Thursday, which honours Christ's Ascension into heaven on the fortieth day after Easter. A rogation is a supplication, or an asking, as in prayer, at the time of a crisis or calamity. The earliest known observance of rogation days occurred in the fifth century when, after a series of devastating earthquakes, the Bishop Mamercus of Vienna directed the people to set aside these days for fasting, prayers and processions. The custom, with Church support, gradually spread from Western Europe and made its appearance in England in the eighth century.

In instituting Rogationtide, the wise Viennese Bishop was successfully employing the same reasoning used by Augustine in his redemption of heathen customs through the bestowal on them of a Christian object. The practices which the Rogation days were replacing were the Roman festivals of *Terminalia* and *Ambarvalia*. The god Terminus was worshipped annually towards the end of February in the form of a sacrifice at boundary markers. *Ambarvalia* was observed on May 29th, when crowds would gather at a Roman territorial boundary and have processions around their crops, holding sticks in their hands to frighten winter away, performing sacrifices and making merry in the anticipation of plentiful harvests and coming summer.

It was because of the precarious state of the crops at this early date in the season that Rogationtide practices have centred on the land. Other than their coincidence in their timing with the fortieth day after Easter, the customs have little about their character or purpose to tie them in with the religious mystery of the Ascension. Rogation days in England became known as Gange days from the Saxon verb *gangen*, to go. On these days the local priest or bishop would lead a procession

BEATING THE BOUNDS IN LONDON.

around the parish boundaries. The practice is most frequently known as **'Beating the Bounds'**, but Chambers advises that alternate names were "processioning, rogationing, perambulating, and ganging the boundaries." The beating was performed, usually with long willow wands, at every boundary marker, be it a stone, a wall or a tree. There were also frequent stops by the priest for a reading from a Psalm, a reminder to his parishioners to give thanks for the fruits of the earth, or admonitions like, "Cursed be he which translateth the bounds and doles of his neighbour."

Unlike the fasting and supplication which attended the original rogations, the later affairs were of considerable ceremony, and included bells and banners and halts for feasting and for the quenching of thirst. Every able member of the village was required to participate in these processions and, in the days before ordnance survey maps, this was a particularly effective way of impressing the parish perimeters on the young. To increase this impression they, and not the markers, were often the ones beaten. In addition, if the boundaries ran through a hedgerow or along a stream, they would be obliged to crawl through the hedge, though it were full of nettles, or to swim the stream. If the marker was a tree or a stone, more often than not, like the earlier Roman sacrifices, a boy's head would be battered against it until it was certain he would never forget its location. There are many stories of houses which lie on the boundary lines through which the crowd would wend its way, using doors or windows as points of entrance or egress, to ensure a continuance of historical boundary rights. There is a case on record in which a noble's carriage was parked exactly on a boundary line in London when a rogation procession approached. The coachman refused to move it on the grounds that his master had ordered him to stay there until his return. To the coachman's consternation, the procession, one by one, churchwardens, parish officers, "cads, sweeps and scavengers," entered the carriage by one door and left it by the other.

The traditions of Rogationtide came to lose most of their religious ties until a revival came about during the last century. In spite of our modern maps and meticulously surveyed borderlines, there are still numerous parishes in which the bounds, but not the boys, are beaten annually. Often the procession is made up of schoolchildren or choirboys, and blessings are said for the crops, the pastures and the waterways. On the whole, this particular revival must be met with an especial commendation. The reminders of ancestral boundaries and habits, of nature and of the Church through Beating the Bounds cannot but be timely ones in our increasingly urbanised and industrialised society.

Ascension Day is the Thursday of Rogation Week, the fifth week after Easter. It commemorates Christ's ascent to heaven having "shewed himself alive after his passion by many infallible proofs, being seen of them forty days, and speaking of the things pertaining to the kingdom of God ... And when he had spoken these things, while they beheld, he was taken up; and a cloud received him out of their sight." (Acts 1:3 and 9.)

Ascension Day never really captured the popular imagination. It is a strange omission that, while elaborate custom and ritual have attached themselves to Christ's birth, death and resurrection, there is so little ceremony associated with the Ascension. And yet, this union with the Father would seem an even further and more joyous step than the Resurrection. Some reflection, however, points to a reason for this apparent enormous oversight in the annual celebrations we have inherited. Earthbound as we are, the occurrences of birth and death become understandable and even commonplace incidents. An eagerness for a conquest of death, as in the Resurrection, makes that event deeply worthy of celebration, even though it be much more difficult to comprehend. But, so long as we are formed of mortal clay, and have not had that spiritual blessing of the Apostles, we are left in perplexity as to how properly to honour a development so far beyond our secular understanding.

Hence, although some Roman Catholic countries mark Ascension Day with a public holiday, in England it is mostly known for the custom of **Well-Dressing**, a practice which owes

THE HALL WELL, TISSINGTON, AS DRESSED FOR ASCENSION DAY.

more to pagan mythology than to its Christian feast day. Spotted throughout the country, but concentrating in Derbyshire and the West, ancient wells are dressed with breathtakingly beautiful mosaics of flowers and leaves. The patterns, put together by experienced craftsmen, usually carry a message along with pictorial designs. Appropriately enough, the tableau often reflects an Ascension motif with words such as "He is gone to glory where we hope to go" or, simply, "He has ascended into heaven." The tradition of dressing wells is generally attributed in this country to medieval days, when people gave thanks for a water supply which had carried them through a plague, like the dreaded Black Death of 1348-9, or through a severe drought. The real origins, however, go back to much earlier pagan worship of water sprites and nymphs, who were thought to control the flow of the life-giving elixir. Seneca admonished the Romans to erect altars and to offer sacrifices at riversides and springs. We have our own Roman example of this which can still be seen at the mineral springs of Bath. In spite of edicts against well-worship by Edgar and Canute in the tenth and eleventh centuries, the practice of going to sacred wells on Ascension Day in order to effect special cures continued to be popular until it was forbidden in the Reformation. Now, many of the wells have been rededicated to saints and, where the well-dressing still takes place, notably at Tissington, Derbyshire, the ceremony has a religious theme, and usually includes a thanksgiving service performed by the local clergy.

May 29, 1660, saw the entry into London of the newly restored Charles II. The day was one of tremendous jubilation after the difficult years of the Commonwealth. Church bells and music filled the air, and crowds thronged the streets, strewing flowers in his path, to welcome him. The date became an annual celebration, and is best known as **Oak Apple Day**, recalling an incident during the Interregnum which caught the fancy of the populace. On September 4, 1651, after the defeat of the Royalist Scottish troops by Cromwell's soldiers at the battle of Worcester, Charles II was obliged to elude capture by the Roundheads through hiding in an oak tree at Boscobel.

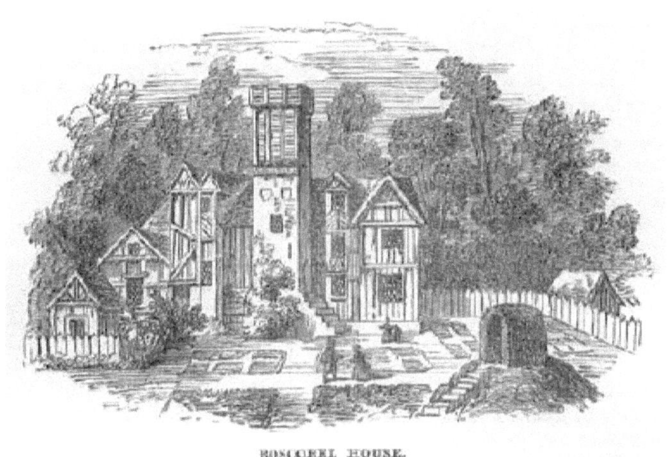

Boscobel House

A suggestion of greenery combined with a date in May was enough of an excuse for more merrymaking. In some villages May Day celebrations, with their garlands, greenery and the Maypole itself, were transferred to the 29th, in the belief that the earlier date had been contaminated through the abstemious Parliamentary bans. It was most usual on this day for oak boughs to be cut early in the morning in the woods, and brought back into the village. These branches would be used to line the streets and to decorate the church, public houses and hones. Now that the tyrannical Parliament was assuredly a phenomenon of the past, loyal subjects displayed their Royalist sympathies by sporting an oaken twig with an oak apple on their clothing.

The Royal Oak also became a popular alehouse sign, and the village pub which hung the largest oak bough on the 29th was guaranteed the heaviest volume of business.

**Coat of Arms sporting the oak
granted to Colonel Careless, who was
the King's companion in the tree**

May has been a month full of festivities. It has traditionally been a restful month in the country. For the farmer, the earth has been prepared and the crops sown by the end of April; so weeding became the biggest chore to face in the month. The husbandman's sheep are out grazing and are not yet ready for shearing or slaughter. The cooler days of the month remind him of the old proverb:

> Shear your sheep in May,
> And shear them all away.

So he is content to sit back, waiting for the reward of his labours, and delighting in the sight of the young lambs frisking, leaping and butting each other in the pastures.

Although the earlier part of the month may still see the appearance of some of last year's carrots and potatoes, there is much new growth for the table by the middle of May. The first fresh and green spinach becomes available, and there are plenty of new asparagus, broccoli, beetroot, cauliflower and large crisp radishes. Rhubarb is ready for desserts and, towards the end of the month, the very earliest of the strawberries add their delightful taste and colour to a meal.

JUNE

Calm weather in June
Sets all in tune.

Although Ovid claimed Juno for this month's namesake, Macrobius is probably more correct in giving that origin to the *Juniores* who, under the direction of Romulus in the first Roman constitution, were charged with the defence of the city. Romulus was the one who originally gave June thirty days, it having had only twenty-six in the earlier Alban calendar. One of these days was later taken away by Numa Pompilius but was subsequently restored by Julius Caesar.

The Saxons, as with other months, used more natural descriptions in naming their June. Among their various terms for it were *Weydmonath*, meaning a month of pasturing livestock; *Braeckmonath*, for breaking the soil; *Woedmonath*, for weeding; and, perhaps most appropriate, *Midsumormonath*, in honour of the critical solstice which occurs later in the month.

June heralds the end of spring. The trees are at their finest of the whole year, the branches and leaves filled out with a new fresh sheen about them. They still have a profusion of blossoms, as well. The lilac, elder, laburnum and chestnut buds have all come out. Below them on the ground we find other flowers providing a riot of colour. Clover fills the meadows with its sweet aroma, a magnet for the busy bee. Many garden vegetables are now in blossom, among the prettiest of which are the bean and pea plants. The ornamental thistle also blooms, as does the foxglove, a favourite of cottage gardens, looking like bright columns of fire pointing to the heavens.

But the flower which most transfigures this month in garden and hedgerow alike is the rose. The beauty of this blossom has been honoured since the most remote antiquity. It is spoken of in Coptic manuscripts and throughout the Old Testament. The apocryphal Wisdom of Solomon's "Let us crown ourselves with rosebuds before they be withered" could certainly have been the inspiration for Herrick's 'Gather ye Rose-buds while ye may." The rose has played a part in the lines of most major English writers including Chaucer, Spenser, Milton and Shakespeare. The latter's Juliet gave the classic line that "a rose by any other name would smell as sweet." It has a very special place in our heritage, as it was chosen to be the royal emblem for England after the Houses of York and Lancaster had put an end to the 30 year Wars of the Roses in the late fifteenth century. During these wars the Yorkist faction is reputed to have worn a white single or semi-double variety of the *Rosa alba* species, more commonly known as the Dog rose, which still beautifies many of our hedgerows. Its fruit, the rose-hip, is rich in vitamin C and began to be collected during the Second World War to make National Rose-Hip Syrup as a substitute for the then hard to come by oranges.

June's balmy days are ideal for pleasant country jaunts, and an attentive walker will note many new insects. The grasshopper makes an appearance, as do other varieties of flies and beetles. One of the commonest sights along a stream or river on a warm June evening is the *ephemera vulgata*, the angler's mayfly or dragonfly. This insect is appropriately named, for its life is truly ephemeral. It comes out of the water at about six in the evening and is often dead before midnight.

That most beloved of insects, the butterfly, follows a cycle which parallels the natural process of flowering plants. At first, like the seed, it is an egg from which the caterpillar emerges, its entrance timed for its meals on spring's abundance of new leaves. Then, when it has had its fill of these, it spins its blanket around itself, waiting in its chrysalis state for that mysterious transformation into a butterfly. Coincident with this awakening are the outbursts of flowers, whose plants have gone through their own metamorphosis by the time June rolls around. Only now, when nature is at her finest, can the delicate butterfly survive, feeding through its proboscis of the fragrant nectar provided by these blooms. Much of this miraculous timing, of course, can be ascribed to sensitivity to temperature shared by flowers and butterflies alike. The lives of both are guided by the sun. The insect closes its wings and many a blossom their petals, at night, or when the sky is gloomy with clouds. When the sun is beaming down, both open wide to receive its beneficial rays.

In the pastoral countryside, June's warm temperature makes it safe for the important task of sheep-shearing. The drudgery of this chore has traditionally been mitigated through making it a ceremony which sometimes includes contests and prizes, which is often followed by a sumptuous feast. John Dyer devoted the longest of his eighteenth century poems, *The Fleece*, to the care of sheep and the making of wool. His poetical instructions regarding the timing of shearing were,

> If verdant elder spreads
> Her silver flowers; if humble daisies yield
> To yellow crowfoot and luxuriant grass,
> Gay shearing time approaches.

One of the country's earliest exports was wool sent to Flemish weavers. Subsequent growth in the wool trade during the Middle Ages made England wealthy and famous for its breeds of sheep. So important was the wool harvest that medieval shepherds were among the most valued of servants on the farms. It was forbidden them to take leave without permission to visit the public house, or to attend fairs, markets or wrestling matches. Not much later a preference was shown for lame shepherds, in the belief that they were unable ever to hurry the treasured stock. Sheep were originally kept primarily for their wool, but their milk was also valued, particularly for the special cheeses made in some districts. The meat was useful, but not held in too high esteem. It wasn't until much later that their manure in the fold came to be appreciated by the farmer, who would let them graze for free on his fallow lands in order that his soil might benefit.

Coinciding with, or just preceding, sheep-shearing is the moveable feast of **Whitsuntide**, which usually falls in late May or early June. Whit Sunday is the seventh following Easter, and honours the descent of the Holy Ghost on the disciples. One of the final things spoken of by Christ was that the disciples would receive the power of the Holy Ghost in the very near future. This experience, a transmission of spiritual force and grace to humanity after the Ascension, must certainly form one of the most critical dates in all Christian history. The baptism of the Apostles by the Spirit has become the lesser of the three pillars in the popular Christian year; the other two being Christmas and Easter. The day is also referred to as Pentecost from the Greek word for fifty, meaning that this experience came to the Apostles on the fiftieth day after the beginning of the harvest.

 As described in Acts 2:1-4, when the Disciples were "all with one accord in one place ... suddenly there came a mighty rushing wind, and it filled all the house where they were sitting. And there appeared unto them cloven tongues like as of fire and it sat upon each of them. And they were all filled with the Holy Ghost, and began to speak with other tongues as the Spirit gave them utterance." This eschatological event sounded the death-knell of the old order and inaugurated a new era in human history. The coming of the Spirit was a sign of the continuity of Christ's presence, in spite, or perhaps because, of the Ascension after the last of the resurrection appearances. This dawn of a higher consciousness in a handful of men certainly merited an unusually solemn remembrance, especially as it held a hopeful promise of its manifestation in others. And yet, as in Ascension Day, our ancestors were at an understandable loss as to how such a mystery could adequately be honoured.

One method was to imitate this baptism by the Spirit with that of water. In fact, the name Whit Sunday comes from *Hwita Sunnandaeg*, or White Sunday, after the great number of white garments worn for baptisms on this date in Saxon times. Whitsun festivals were observed with much more ceremony during medieval days than afterwards. The nobility of Western Europe were particular celebrants of the occasion, if contemporary legends are to be believed. Sir Thomas Malory's fifteenth century romance of King Arthur gives his hero "a custome, that at the high feast of Pentecost especially, afore al other high feasts in the yeare, he would not goe that day to meat until he had heard or seene some great adventure or mervaile. And for that costum all manner of strange adventures came before King Arthur at that feast afore all other feasts."

The **Whitsun-Ale** evolved as another feature of this day. A parochial meeting and feast were arranged, and all parishioners and churchwardens would lay aside disputes and commemorate the occasion in friendship. This celebration was, no doubt, based on the accord which the Apostles had achieved during their memorable Pentecost, but also may owe some of its origins to the Eucharistic fellowship dinners, spoken of by Paul, which had been enjoyed by the infant Christian community.

Ale was such a common drink not so long ago that it appeared as part of the sobriquet for different festive dinners, including the **Church-Ale**, the Lamb Ale, the Clerk's-Ale and the Bride-Ale, the last of which terms has come down to us in the word 'bridal'.

Whitsun-Ales and Church-Ales were generally held in a barn or on the north side of the churchyard, where there were traditionally fewer graves to interfere with the revelry. Many parish churches also had a church-house in which the feast could be prepared. But before this merry-making could take place, the Whit Sunday service, in a church decorated with birch or yew boughs, would be attended by all participants, and each would make his communion. Afterwards, a Lord and Lady of the Ale were elected, and various attendants chosen to wait on them. These servants were usually comprised of a steward, a sword-bearer, a mace-bearer, a page, a jester and train-bearers. Each was costumed in bright colours and adorned with bells and ribbons. A bower made of garlands, green branches and ribbons would be built against the side of the church to house the thrones. This had been condoned by Augustine, but on the condition that the object of such festivities be that of raising alms. Accordingly, the beer and sometimes a portion of a Whit Cake were supplied and sold by the churchwardens with proceeds going to the parish poor or to church repairs. But, as time marched on, the pious object of the occasion took a secondary place to the boisterous feast. Maypoles, Morris Dancers and Hobby Horses were added at some locations, and a gaudily costumed Fool would be given license to berate the celebrants with his witticisms, emphasising his comments with blows from a pig's bladder as a means of increasing the general merriment. Games and sports also took place, and included wrestling matches, shooting galleries and greased poles. The ale provided was traditionally stronger than usual and, as a consequence, attracted many customers who, we suspect, may have had ulterior motives in their generous contributions to the parish coffers.

Inevitably, so much enjoyment came under the harsh scrutiny of the Puritans. Our sixteenth century Stubbes, casting his jaundiced eye on the Whitsuntide merrymaking, wrote the following:

"...then they have their Hobby-horses, dragons and other Antiques, togither with their baudie Pipers and thundering Drummers to strike up the devils daunce withal. Then, marche these heathen company towards the Church and the Church-yard, their pipers pipeing, their drummers thundering, their strumps dauncing, their bells iyngling, their handkerchefs swinging about their heds like madmen, their hobbie-horses and other monsters skirmishing amongst the rout; and in this sorte they go into the Church (I say) & into the Church (though the Minister be at praier or preaching), dancing & swinging their handkerchiefs over their heds in the Church, like devils incarnate, with such a confuse noise, that no man can hear his own voice. Then, the foolish people they looke, they stare, they laugh, they fleer, and mount upon fourmes and pews to see these goodly pagents solemnised in this sort. Then, after this, about the Church they go again, and againe, & so foorth into the church-yard where they have commonly their Sommerhaules, their bowers, arbors and banqueting houses set up, wherein they feast, banquet and daunce at that day, & (peradventure) all night too. And thus these terrestriall furies spend the Saboath day."

The Puritans, along with their later Nonconformist brethren finally took their inexorable toll on the Whitsun festival during the eighteenth and nineteenth centuries. It slowly died out in one village after another, and parish proceeds gradually grew instead from pew rentals and other sources. The Whitsun-Ale was too strong, and the reaction was the echo of an earlier moralist, Paul, who, in his first letter to the Corinthians (11:20-22), chastised them for turning the agape, or love-feast, into a gluttonous and dissipated outing:

"When ye come together therefore into one place, this is not to eat the Lord's supper. For in eating every one taketh before others his own supper: and one is hungry, and another is drunken. What? have ye not houses to eat and drink in? or despise ye the church of god, and shame them that have not? What shall I say to you? shall I praise you in this? I praise you not."

The religious importance of Whit Sunday was such that a holiday was tacked onto it and a variety of customs clustered around this date. **Whitsun Mystery Plays** used to be a common feature during this week. The most famous example took place in Chester and was an ambitious undertaking, for the plays there sought to portray the whole story of the Bible in twenty-five acts performed over the Monday, Tuesday and Wednesday of Whit-week. Mystery Plays are thought to have originated on the Continent in the tenth century and to have gradually spread throughout Europe. As with other festivals, some clerics viewed the plays with misgivings, but others, including the eminent Luther, approved. The plays were laced with moral admonitions and filled a large gap in popular education by instructing the people in Biblical history. During the dark ages, even in the unlikely event one was literate, the Bible was a prohibited book to lay readers. The pageants thus shed a broad light on religious history and prophecy, and were something of a palliative substitute experience for the original Feast of the Tongues of Fire.

The Chester Plays were first written by a monk at Chester Abbey around the year 1300. The separate acts included such stunning titles as *Creation*, *The Flood*, *The Harrowing of Hell*, *Passion*, *Antichrist* and, for the last in the series, a sobering *Doomsday*. One of the plays, *The Fall of Lucifer*, is thought to have inspired John Milton's *Paradise Lost*. The organisers followed the sensible procedure of performing the plays in all of the principal streets in order to bring the stories to as many as possible and to prevent excessive crowding. The stages were two-tiered structures set on wheels. The acting was done on the top storey, while costume-changing took place on the lower covered floor. When one act finished, the stage would be moved to another street, while a second one took its place for the next act. In addition to the unusual entertainment the performances provided, a further inducement to attend came from days of grace which were automatically granted to members of the audience. The spectacle of the Chester Mystery Plays reached its zenith during Elizabethan days, and then waned and died out in the middle of the seventeenth century. We must now look to the Oberammergau Passion Play for the most notable relic of this type of festival.

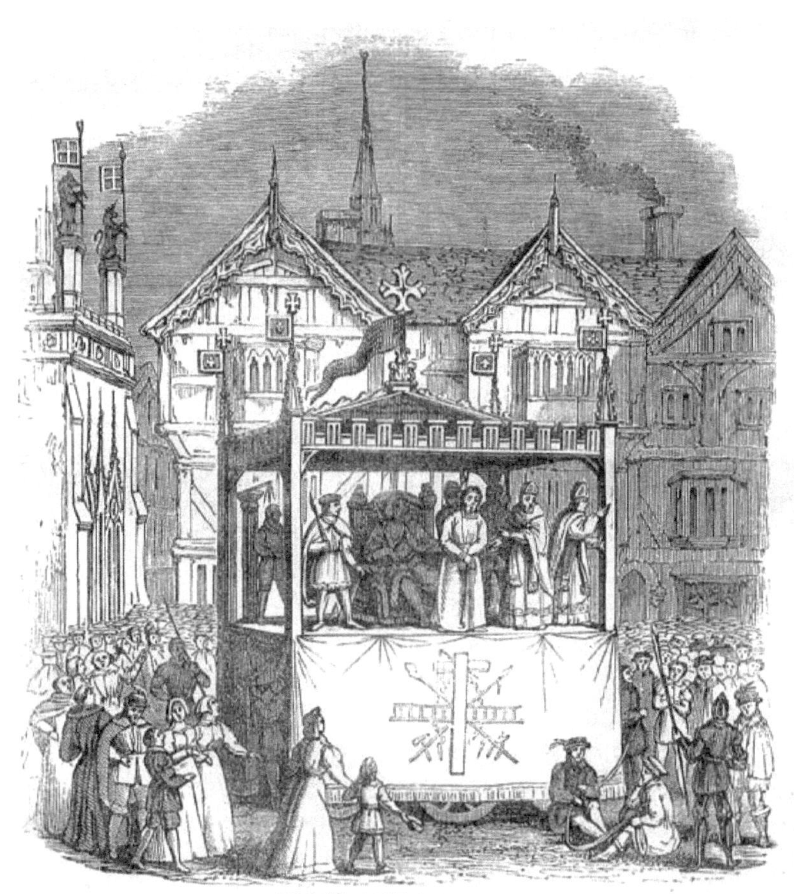

CHESTER MYSTERY PLAYS.

The curious Whit Monday custom of the Dunmow Flitch is still practiced at Great **Dunmow** in Essex. A **flitch**, the whole side of a pig, or a gammon is awarded to a couple who have been married for more than a year and who have had no disagreements or desires to separate during that time. Originally staged at the Priory of Little Dunmow, the custom received early mention in Langland's *Piers Plowman* and from Chaucer's wife of Bath. In pre-Reformation days, the Prior, his fellow monks and the villagers of Little Dunmow tested the applicant and neighbours of his to determine his worthiness to receive the flitch. Now the jury is made up of an equal number of bachelors and spinsters who, although possessing no experience of marriage themselves, must soon acquire an excellent insight into the state of wedded bliss, as well as into its possible attendant pitfalls. In the early practice, the applicant had to kneel on two large and sharp stones which lay near the church door, and swear to the following oath, as related by Philip Morant in his *History and Antiquities of the County of Essex* (1768):

"You shall swear by custom of confession,
That you ne'er named nuptial transgression;
Nor since you were married man and wife
By household brawls or contentious strife,
Or otherwise in bed or at board,
Offended each other in deed or word:
Or since the parish clerk said amen
Wished yourselves unmarried again;
Or in a twelve-month and a day
Repented not in thought in any way,
But continued through in thought and desire,
As when you joined hands in holy quire.
If to these conditions, without all fear
Of your own accord you will freely swear,
A whole gammon of bacon you shall receive,
And bear it hence with love and good leave;
For this is our custom at Dunmow well known,
Though the pleasure be ours, the bacon's your own."

Feminists will be glad to learn that by the eighteenth century the wife was also required to attest to her conjugal felicity. Previous to that, the husband's words on the matter were considered sufficient. Thomas Shakeshaft, an Essex wool-comber, and his wife Ann won the flitch in 1751 and were carried in the Dunmow Chair in procession through the town with the flitch held aloft before them. Thomas and his wife were resourceful enough to make a large profit from selling slices of their prize to many of the five thousand spectators who attended the ceremony.

The custom is known to have been practiced at some other locations in England and in France, but none received the renown of Dunmow's flitch. The same tradition was observed at Wychner in Staffordshire during the reign of Edward III (1327-1377). The oath used there was a little more sombre, and is quoted in *Howitt's*

Pictorial Calendar of the Seasons from Sir William Dugdale's *The Baronage of England* (1675):

> "....that I, A site I wedded B my wife, and sythe I hadde hyr in my keeping and at my wylle by a yere and a day, after our mariage, I wold not have chaunged for none other descended of gretter lynage, slepyng ne waking, at noo time. And yf the seid B were sole, and I sole, I wolde take her to be my wyfe before alle the wymen of the worlde, of what condiciones soever they be, good or evylle; as helpe me God and his seyntis, and this fleshe and all fleshes."

The Dunmow Procession 1751

Although lapsing at times for whole generations, the presentation of the Dunmow Flitch has endured for more than 600 years. It is hoped that the longer gaps were due more to a mean disposition on the part of the Lord of the Manor, who had inherited the custom from the Priory, than to the rarity of harmonious marriages. Its present popularity stands out as a happy, though somewhat jocular, reaffirmation of wedded virtues in these days of laxer morals and soaring divorce statistics.

One Devonshire Whit Monday custom owes more to Old Testament sacrifices than to the Apostles' Pentecostal experience. This is the **Ram Roasting Fair** at Kingsteinton, where the roast male lamb is distributed to the attending crowd. There are games, Maypole dancing and other revelry to participate in while the roasting is performed on an outdoor spit. The custom is thought to have as its origins a Celtic pagan sacrifice aimed at bringing back the flow of water to an important spring which had suddenly dried up. Presumably Augustine's teachings initiated the part where the meat is distributed to the villagers. Thus, instead of being a propitiatory offering to an earlier water deity, the festival is now directed to the common good.

Two other Whitsuntide customs, observed in Gloucestershire, acknowledge the natural calendar through awarding prizes of cheese, an important product for their rural economy. Both are reputedly connected with securing grazing rights. The first of these is celebrated on Whit Sunday at the parish church of St. Briavels and is said to date from the thirteenth century. Before the middle of the nineteenth century, **bread and cheese** were flung from the galleries of the church to the parishioners, who would scramble for them below. Subsequently the prizes were tossed down from the church tower, until it became evident that the scramble was incurring excessive damage to the gravestones in the churchyard. After that the distribution was moved to a nearby lane where it continues to this day.

The second custom is **Cheese-Rolling**, and used to take place on Whit Monday in the Brockworth parish on Cooper's Hill. Now, like many other Whit Monday traditions, it is normally observed on the Spring Bank Holiday. In this celebration a cheese encased in a wooden container is rolled down the hill on the count of three. At the next count, four, the contestants race after it and the first to reach it is awarded it as a prize. It has attained such local popularity that there are now as many as five or six different races run each year. The steepness of Cooper's Hill adds to the fun, for the spectators are more often than not treated to the sight of many of the contestants rolling down the hill after their reward.

Trinity Sunday succeeds Whitsuntide and is the last way post of the moveable feasts until we reach the first Sunday of Advent in late November or early December. Up to 27 Sundays can fall between these two dates, and they are known simply as Sundays after Trinity or as Sundays after Pentecost. The annual commemoration of Holy Trinity in England is thought to have been started by Thomas Becket, the martyred Archbishop of Canterbury, towards the end of the twelfth century. The concept of the Trinity implies an indivisible individuality. In spite of the apparent unfathomable mystery involved in this idea of simultaneous union and separateness, Holy Trinity has become one of the most popular of all names for English churches and countless analogous architectural symbols, representative of Three in One, can be found woven decoratively into these buildings.

Three Oxfordshire villages used to honour Trinity Monday with a **Lamb Ale** celebrating in a fashion very similar to the earlier Whitsun-Ales. The principle differences distinguishing the Lamb Ale were a Lord and Lady of the Lamb and, of course, a fare of roast lamb which was enjoyed by the parishioners. One interesting feature of the Lamb Ale observed in Kidlington was the means by which the Lady of the Lamb was chosen. The candidates would have their thumbs tied together behind their backs, and the lady became the contestant who succeeded in catching the doomed lamb with her mouth. The earlier boisterous processions and merrymaking which attended the Lamb Ales have died out, and the most notable survival of the festival is in the village of Kirtlington, in a somewhat modified version.

The Thursday after Trinity Sunday, **Corpus Christi Day**, was an occasion of great celebration in pre-Reformation England, and continues to be an important feast day in Roman Catholic countries. Its full name in English is the Feast of the Most Holy Body of Christ, and it has honoured the Holy Eucharist at the Last Supper since the feast was first instituted by a Cistercian nun at Liege in the thirteenth century. In medieval England it included a procession, through the church and nearby streets, of priests bearing the church plate and consecrated bread, others carrying figures of favourite saints, and groups representing the prominent local guilds. As in so many other calendar festivals, these processions and the mystery and miracle plays which followed them were too close to idolatry and amusement to survive under the stern eyes of the post-Reformation Protestant clergy.

Before the change in the calendar, June 11, **St. Barnabas' Day**, marked an ominous seasonal milestone, since on it fell the summer solstice. Barnabas was a fellow-worker of St. Paul, and was later stoned to death in Cyprus for his faith. The now nearly forgotten proverb was duly coined:

> Barnaby bright,
> The longest day and the shortest night.

In addition to its famous thorn, the grounds of the abbey at Glastonbury were supposed also to boast a walnut tree which was said almost always to come into bud on St. Barnabas' feast day. But we need not venture as far as Glastonbury for such wonders. If we are not too inured to miracles, every field and garden present us with prodigies of natural transfiguration around this date.

The seasons have advanced far enough for June to give us not only its harvest of fleece, but also that of hay. Tradition deemed Barnaby's Day to be the first of haymaking. The harvesting of this crop used to be one of the most picturesque of all rural scenes and, when viewed from a comfortable distance, typified to urban minds, especially those of artists and writers, the results of an intelligent and harmonious interaction between man and the elements which surround him. Manual haymaking on a large scale is now almost beyond living memory, but many of us will have read descriptions, or seen pictures or films, of it. It was a communal effort, with lines of men moving down the rows and swinging their scythes in unison, transforming the sea of waving grass into fallen swathes. These were gathered with huge wooden rakes into long windrows and left to dry in the summer sun. After a few days they were turned over to complete the drying process. "Make hay while the sun shines" was no idle dictum. Finally, the windrows would be rolled like snowballs into great haycocks which were trimmed at the top for rain-proofing. It was strenuous work in the heat of summer, and the labourers often took a daily ration of beer with them in 'plough bottles', small wooden casks, to help quench their thirst. After the hay was pitched onto hay wagons in enormous loads, it was taken behind straining and sweating horses to the rick yard. The hayricks, looking like perfectly formed grass houses, were erected, each with a carefully fashioned thatch roof to protect the harvest from inclement weather.

Gradually, however, the processes became automated. The mechanical mower replaced the scythe. The wooden rake fell by the wayside in favour of the automatic swathe turner. Pick-up balers and elevators removed the need for the pitchfork, while the tractor supplanted the workhorse. Finally, by 1945, the combine harvester came into standard use, uniting in one machine most of the tasks performed by the separate ones and virtually eliminating human participation in haymaking. All we are left with now is the colour and scent of the newly mown hay.

This is progress, but such advances invariably reveal a second edge to their sword. The machines are called 'labour-saving' but they have not resulted in any significant increase in leisure, except for those who are out of work. Hay indubitably costs less to make mechanically, but the operator of the combine harvester still works as long a day as did his manual predecessors. There are other even more important implications. Where is the communal effort? Where is the joyful and richly deserved festival marking the meaningful step taken in the seasons? How are we to adequately compensate for the loss of experiential training and the intensive rhythmic workout which were provided naturally by the variety of manual tasks involved in haymaking and other forfeited agricultural chores? Most of all, one wonders where today's labourer, in or out of work, is to find that daily bread so indispensable to the nurturing of a spiritual maturing.

June 24 arrives towards the end of haymaking and represents **Midsummer's Day**, although the true solstice falls about three days earlier. In the Church it is celebrated as the **Nativity of St. John the Baptist** (implying that the baby John was six months old when the infant Jesus was born). It was a quarter day in England, when rents became due, based like the Druidic cycle, on the equinoxes and solstices.

The celebrations for this day began on its eve with huge **bonfires** being lit on hills in the country, or on village greens in towns. Googe quotes the poet Naogeorgus:

> Then doth the joyfull feast of John
>   The Baptist take his turne
> When bonfires great, with loftie flame,
>   In every towne doe burn...

In the cities, until Henry VIII put an end to the practice in 1539, people **paraded with torches** to keep a watch after sunset. These processions were as many as two thousand strong in London and must have made an impressive sight in the days before streetlights. After Henry VIII's death, the marching was revived in 1548, but fell into disuse again shortly afterwards.

At other locations an old wheel would have straw from the hay harvest twisted around it. This would be taken to a prominent hilltop at nightfall, set alight and rolled down. If observed from a distance, it would look much like the symbol it was meant to represent on this date: The round blaze of the sun itself falling in the heavens. In addition to its reminder of the celestial drama, it was believed this practice was indispensible in warding off otherwise inevitable misfortunes.

One of the most notable St. John's Eve bonfire practices occurs in Cornwall, where bonfires are lit in a chain stretching from the western to eastern tips of the county. The Federation of Old Cornwall Societies revived this custom in the late 1920s. At the individual fires in the chain a Master of Ceremonies starts the evening with the words:

> Now to the pyre
> At once set fire,
> Let the flames aspire
> In God's high name!

A Lady of Flowers, appointed by the member society concerned, lights the fire and throws herbs and a garland of flowers onto it. In spite of the Christian overtones, bonfire customs were originally pagan, and surviving records indicate that **Midsummer's Eve fires** were a feature not only of the Druidic faith, but also of the faiths existing in ancient Egypt and in India. It was believed that great fires on earth would encourage the waning powers of the sun.

Up until the Middle Ages, bonfires in many locations were connected with a variety of superstitions. Cattle were driven through the embers to prevent murrain, herbs would be burnt ritually, and young people were wont to leap over the flames to bring themselves luck and to ward off evil. The Puritans, quoting Scripture, condemned these rites, for in Leviticus God warns Moses against letting his people's seed pass through fire and, again, in the second book of Kings, Manasseh makes his son go through flames with the express purpose of angering the Lord.

It is John the Baptist's link with water to which some attribute the **Well-Dressing** which occurs near Midsummer's Day in two Derbyshire villages. However, as in similar Ascension Day practices, these traditions have their roots in much earlier pagan and classical lore. Two dressed wells are blessed at Buxton on the Thursday nearest June 24. One of Buxton's wells was Roman in origin, and its water was popular for its supposed healing power up until 1538, when one of Cromwell's agents put an end to that kind of worship. A Wells Festival Queen reigns over the present-day

ST ANNE'S WELL, BUXTON, DECORATED.

Buxton celebrations which are thought to have been revived in 1840 to commemorate the Duke of Devonshire's supplying of this spa town with piped-in water. Another Derbyshire village, Youlgrave, **dresses its old public taps** on the Saturday nearest St. John the Baptist's Nativity Day.

Other **St. John's Eve** practices were carried out by unmarried maidens, as methods of divining the identities of their future husbands. One of these customs involved 'Midsummer Men', in which a stalk of orpine, a herbaceous and purple-flowering plant, was set into lumps of clay and left overnight. When the maiden awoke in the morning, she would eagerly check to see which way the stalk had wilted in order to discover whether or not her lover was faithful.

Brand quotes a number of these superstitions which had appeared in number 56 of *The Connoisseur*, a periodical which came out in the mid-nineteenth century:

> "I and my two sisters tried the dumb-cake together: you must know, two must make it, two must bake it, two break it, and the third put it under each of their pillows (but you must not speak a word all the time) and then you will dream of the man you are to have. This we did: and to be sure I did nothing all night but dream of Mr. Blossom.
>
> "The same night, exactly at twelve o'clock, I sowed hemp-seed in our back yard and said to myself, 'Hemp-seed I sow, Hemp-seed I hoe, and he that is my true-love come after me and mow.' Will you believe me? I looked back and saw him behind me, as plain as eyes could see him. After that, I took a clean shift and wetted it, and turned it wrong-side out, and hung it to the fire upon the back of a chair; and very likely my sweetheart would have come and turned it right again (for I heard his step), but I was frightened and could not help speaking, which broke the charm. I like wise stuck up two Midsummer Men, one for myself and one for him. Now if his had died away, we should never have come together, but I assure you, his blowed and turned to mine. Our maid Betty tells me, that if I go backwards, without speaking a word, into the garden, upon Midsummer's Eve, and gather a rose, and keep it in a clean sheet of paper, without looking at it till Christmas Day, if will be as fresh as in June; and if I stick it in my bosom, he that is to be my husband will come and take it out."

Other beliefs were connected with St. John' wort and the fern. Young men would go out at night to try to catch the almost invisible fern seed on plates, without touching the plant itself. If they were successful, these 'supernatural' seeds were supposed to give them the power of invisibility. Much of the plot and humour of Shakespeare's *A Midsummer Night's Dream* is based on the supposition that this particular fancy comes magically true. As in St. Mark' Eve, two months earlier, it was similarly believed that if one fasted and sat up all night in the churchyard, one would see the spirits of those parishioners who would die in the next year come to the church door.

Stonehenge is one memorial to Midsummer's Day which has come to us almost from time out of mind, and in its rugged obstinacy impresses us with the significance of this date more than all the marching watches, bonfires and love divinations put together. The name by which we call this monument is relatively recent, for it is Saxon meaning 'hanging stones', but the origins of the circle are thought to date from about 3000 BC. Stonehenge acts as a calendar, a necessary tool in both pagan and modern religions, keeping track of sacred festival dates during the year. The Druids entered Britain as late as the third century before Christ; hundreds of years after this structure had been completed. However, it is the present-day Church of the **Druid** Universal Bond, claiming to be a relative of those first Druids in England, which many connect with **Stonehenge**, due to the **dawn ritual**s they held there through part of the latter half of the twentieth century.

The day on which we enjoy the maximum benefit from the sun is an ominous turning point in the year. After this we move towards increasing darkness and bleak winter. As a consequence, the principal festivities which associated themselves naturally with Midsummer's Day were lamentations for the dying solar diety. Perhaps for this reason, the early church chose June 24 for the feast day of the Nativity of St. John the Baptist, transforming an occasion for dread to one of joy. For the angels have told us in Luke "many shall rejoice at his birth." The celebration of the Nativity of St. John the Baptist is an exception in the round of saints' days, since almost all other ones mark the anniversaries of their deaths. The first step towards the Good News, placed strategically, as it were, on a day naturally fit for sorrow, highlights the seeming paradox in religion's essential message through interpreting the death of temporal hope as the birth of a spiritual one. The combination suggests a further meaning. The Christian associates water with St. John the Baptist. But, for the pagan, Midsummer's Day was celebrated with flame; torches and bonfires on earth in imitation of the great celestial blaze. The ideas together bring home a truer sense of the meanings behind the aeons of Midsummer's Day festivities and the centuries of Christian baptisms. For, on this day, more than on any other in the entire year, the earth itself is baptised by fire. Reason leads us to conclude that a baptism must be a mystery of union, bringing with it at least as much of birth in one sense as it does of death in another. Such a conclusion acts as a strong reminder of why our ancestors placed such importance on Midsummer's Day festivities. It is an opportunity, provided naturally once a year, on which one can struggle with the ideas of death and rebirth, as well as being a celestial event of such magnitude that each of us cannot help but marvel at the awesome workings of the heavens.

Rush-bearing

Five days after St. John's Nativity is the feast day of St. Peter, the first in a long line of Bishops of Rome, who was martyred on a cross by Nero in 68 AD. Rush-bearing and hay-strewing customs are traditionally associated in England with the period on or near **St. Peter's feast day**. **Rushes were strewn** in churches, usually once a year, to protect the parishioners from the cold stone or earthen floors.

The practice is still ceremonially kept up at a few locations. In Barrowden, in what used to be Rutlandshire, rushes are brought into the parish church on St. Peter's Eve and left there for a week. At Warcop, Westmoreland (now Cumbria), the strewing of rushes has been replaced by a procession into the church of children wearing floral crowns and **carrying rush crosses** on June 29. The crowns and crosses are left to decorate the church until the next year.

Appropriately timed to coincide with the end of June's haymaking, **fresh hay** is taken to the church at Wingrave in Buckinghamshire on the first Sunday after St. Peter's Day, adding its meaningful golden colour and rich aroma to the day's services.

In addition to the vegetables the year has already shown us, June brings a bigger variety of further ones, as well as a number of dessert fruits.

With the sheep shorn and the hay harvested, June usually closes on a note of rural satisfaction. Although the sun is now shining for ever-decreasing periods, real summer weather is almost always finally upon us, and the heat of July and August is still to come, promising an adequate growth and then harvest of other crops.

JULY

***If the first of July be rainy weather
'twill rain more or less for four weeks together.***

The Roman's original name for this month was *Quintilis*, as it took fifth place in their year. Although it had thirty-six days in the Alban Calendar, these were reduced to thirty-one by Romulus and then to thirty by Numa. Being Julius Caesar's natal month, *Quintilis* was also his favourite, and so, several centuries after Numa, he restored its lost day, making it as long as the longest of the other months. After his death, Mark Anthony renamed the month July in honour of Caesar's family name. The connection of Julius's name with the hottest and brightest month of the year also acted as a clear implication that, crowned symbolically by the sun, Caesar had been emperor of the world.

July was the first month of the Celtic year, and its natural associations gave rise to several names for it by our Saxon forefathers. Verstegan tells us they knew it both as *Hey Monath* and as *Maed Monath*; the former referring to their mowing and harvesting of hay during this month, and the latter to the richly blossoming meadows. Other sources claim they also knew it as *Hen Monath*, meaning foliage month, and as *Lida Aftera*, meaning the second Lida, or the second month of the sun's descent, as June had sometimes been called *Lida Erra*, the first month of the sun's descent.

July used to be noteworthy from an astronomical point of view. The period from July 3 to August 11 was known as the Dog-days, as it was during this time that the star Canicula (Sirius), or Little Dog, rose and set with the sun. Since, at that time, the appearance of the Dog Star coincided with the intense heat experienced during this period, some disease and superstition began to be associated with it. The notions connected with these days were apparently Egyptian in origin. The Dog Star at that time also coincided with the overflow of the Nile and the resulting fertility of the land bordering it. Other nations were wont to look at the Dog Star less favourably. In Rome, its ascendance meant that the wine in their cellars would ferment, the seas would boil and that dogs would go mad with the heat. In

England, the effect of July's heat on dogs caused magistrates of different towns to order them to be muzzled around the first of July. The rising of Sirius is not, of course, tied to our solar calendar and, as a result, has lost its earlier associations with July's heat.

Just as July stands furthest from January in the cycle of the year, so is its weather the opposite of our first month's. Invariably, January is our coldest month, while July is our hottest, even though the sun's power began to wane after the summer solstice. The onslaught of heat has an impressive effect on nature. Plants and flowers which bloomed during May and June begin to dry out and wither. Their places are rapidly taken by new ones which glory in July's heat. The red poppy blooms now, as does the marigold, goldenrod and sunflower. The crimson-coloured pimpernel, which can be seen, has been called the shepherd's clock, as it opens at about seven in the morning and closes around noon. Another sobriquet it has had is "the poor man's weatherglass", as it also closes up when it is about to rain. July additionally gives a blossoming of camomile, agrimony and wood botany, all often used in tea-making.

Although much of our wildlife seeks shade, or the refreshment of a stream, during this heat, insect life becomes especially active. Since most insects come back to life in the spring and die or go dormant in one form or another during the autumn, it is vital that they make the most of their summer. Bees ransack the flowers, while dragonflies seem to hover motionlessly over their ponds. The industrious ant is very visible in July and, towards the end of this month, male and female ants are expelled from their old ant-hills by the genderless labourers. The males soon die, but the females, through digging a new home and depositing their eggs, begin fresh colonies. Another of July's creatures, the parasitic gadfly is a pest to horses and other livestock with its bites, justifying the namesake given to its human counterpart.

The heat during this month seems to have a curious effect on birds. Many of them, including the red-breasted robin and the wren, are virtually silent, in contrast to their noisy activities in the spring and again later in the early autumn. The chaffinch, with its bold white stripes on its wings, is an exception, starting its song very early in the morning. Young swallows and martins, which hatched in the spring, gather together in the trees to try out their wings, often becoming dinner for birds of prey before they achieve sufficient proficiency in flight. A few of the migratory birds begin heading south. One of these is the flycatcher, whose young sometimes start off their long journey as early as a fortnight after leaving their nests.

In the pastoral countryside there is still some washing and shearing of sheep going on. About a week used to elapse between these two activities, allowing the wool to dry out and become oily again to make it easier to cut. In some English breeds, as much as fifteen pounds of wool is sheared from a single sheep. Because shearing sheep is necessarily a labour-intensive chore, the feast following its completion is often still in evidence. Such post shearing celebrations are a happy and reminiscent heritage from the earliest days of shearing. A similar feast, hosted by Nabal, an owner of three thousand sheep, is mentioned in chapter 25 of the first Old Testament book of *Samuel*.

The farmer is busy harvesting different of his crops which have by now ripened in July's heat. Flax and hemp are pulled, their fibrous stalks used to make linen, canvas and rope. In northern England, the hay becomes ready and is taken in. Although August is recognised as the harvest month for the important corn crop, in some southern locations it is ready to be reaped by the end of July.

Because of the overlapping harvests of hay in June and in early July, and of corn in late July and in August, much of this month's festivals borrow from those which are usually associated with the two months bordering it. Different rural customs of early July are based on the end of June's Midsummer's Day and hay-strewing, while customs at the end of the month are reminders of August's Lammastide.

By the Julian calendar, July 5 is **Midsummer's Day, Old Style**. It is still celebrated a such at the village of Whalton, Northumberland, where the villagers dance around great **fires** which are lit on Old Midsummer's Eve, July 4. These are believed to date back at least to Celtic times.

Two other customs also observe Midsummer's Day, Old Style. The first is **Bawming the Thorn**, which is celebrated most years in

Appleton Thorn, Cheshire. Bawming infers a sacred decoration. The object decorated in this case is a thorn tree which grows in the middle of the town. The first such tree so venerated was reputed to have been an offshoot of Glastonbury's Holy Thorn, planted in the town in 1125. After a procession through the town, the tree is decorated with flags, flowers and ribbons. Today, there is a parade through the town and, as in Maypole ceremonies, schoolchildren dance in a ring around the thorn and a Bawming song is sung. The earlier festivities and the ensuing boisterous partying which associated itself with the annual ritual eventually drew too rowdy a crowd from the surrounding neighbourhood, and the custom lapsed at times in the 1900s. Although the thorn has either died or been destroyed at different times, it has always been replaced. With its Glastonbury association, one might imagine that the Bawming the Thorn custom would indisputably have Christian roots, but the connection of pagan-styled tree worship coupled with Midsummer's Day suggests something altogether more ancient.

The other custom which also uses Midsummer's Day, Old Style, takes place at Tynwald Hill on the Isle of Man. On July 5 each year, the **preceding year's laws**, which have been passed by the Manx Parliament, must be **proclaimed** from this hill. In the past they were read in full in both Manx and English, but now only their names and summaries are heard. Without this reading new laws would not be legal on the Isle of Man. It seems a strange custom today, but in the times when most were illiterate, how else was news to be communicated effectively? Also, if we consider the reverence in which our ancestors, both pagan and Christian, held the new solar year, we can understand the importance of bringing forward the newest of the old laws so that their effect could be felt or heard by the dying sun, which would still bring the harvests, upon which everyone depended to see them through another winter. The name Tynwald is Norse, meaning a place where a general meeting is held. The annual Tynwald ceremony dates from the time during which the Vikings held the island. Although the earliest record of this custom dates from 1417, it is undoubtedly much older.

During July, more often at some of England's more northerly latitudes, there occur a few customs connected with hay which are reminiscent of St. Peter's Day on June 29. Some locations in Leicestershire until at least recently **strew newly mown hay** in their churches on the Thursday following Midsummer's Day, Old Style. At Old Weston Church in Cambridge, **hay** is also **laid down** on the Sunday nearest July 15, St. Swithin's Day. The hay for this church is supposed to have come from a bequest of the land on which it is grown, which was made by a parishioner who hoped the hay would help dull the noisy and irritating sound of boots heard in the church aisles.

Further north, at Ambleside, in the Lake District, usually on the last Saturday in July, there is a **procession** through the town **bearing garlands made of rushes**, which goes to the church where a special service is held.   Afterwards, gingerbread is distributed to the children in the congregation. The last Saturday in July would be the one nearest St. Anne's Day, which was named in honour of the mother of the Blessed Virgin Mary.

Earlier on in the month, there was a **Lot Meadow Mowing** ceremony which took place at Yarnton in Oxfordshire. In this ceremony, two meadows were divided into strips and lots for them were drawn by freeholders of Yarnton and its neighbouring parishes. Those who own the rights to the hay-mowing could sell their crop by auction on, or near, June 29, St. Peter's Day. The draw was held soon after, early in July, at eight o'clock on a morning. Up until early in the nineteenth century, when the winner of the lot had to harvest his portion with a scythe in one day, there used to be a fair connected with the ancient ceremony. However, the unruly crowds which were drawn to it resulted in a termination of the festivities. The custom, though, was been kept up until fairly recently, but the harvesting today is done with tractors, and so now is dealt with as more straightforward farming business.

Although July is a busy month for the farmer, there is usually something of a lull between the harvest of hay and that of corn. This pause, coupled with the fine weather the month invariably has, gave rise to fairs being enjoyed during the gap. A good number of these fairs developed in the days before store-bought goods were readily available to country folk, and hence they served an important function in allowing these people to buy and sell home-made crafts and home-grown produce. Some of the fairs appear to have been very ancient in origin, and a few fell on or near Midsummer's Day, Old Style.

Many have been discontinued, but one which survived in the **Horn Fair**, celebrated at Ebernoe, in Sussex, on July 25, the feast day of St. James the Great. One of the main attractions to the Horn Fair is a cricket match played by Ebernoe against some other nearby village. Another feature is the roasting of a whole horned sheep in a pit. As many of the participants as is possible help in basting the sheep, as tradition has it that will bring luck. The sheep's head and horns are extended outside of the pit of embers during the roasting to prevent damage to them. Later on, the batsman of the cricket match who has scored the most runs for the winning team is presented with this head and its horns as his prize. The Ebernoe Horn Fair has been celebrated now for at least several centuries. There are a few other horn fairs observed at other locations on different dates. The fact that in some of those the participants wear the horns might be an indication that the annual Horn Fair at Ebernoe could have earlier pre-Christian roots. Perhaps it originated as a pagan rite, a means of giving thanks for a successful hunt.

The Fairlop Oak

Another fair, with much more recent origins, was that of the **Fairlop Oak Festival**, which was observed on the first Friday of July at Hainault Forest in Essex. Two centuries ago, this forest boasted of an enormous oak tree, which was reputed to have had a circumference around its trunk of thirty-six feet. Daniel Day, an eighteenth century pump-maker, so admired this prodigious tree that, together with some friends, he began having an annual dinner of bacon and beans under it. Chambers adds that,

"By and by, the neighbours caught Mr. Day's spirit, and came in multitudes to join his festivities. As a necessary consequence, trafficking people   came to sell refreshments on the spot; afterwards commerce in hard and soft wares found its way thither; shows and tumbling followed; in short, a   regular fair was at last concentrated around the Fairlop Oak..."

The story goes that, much later, when Mr. Day was an old man, the famous oak lost one of its main branches and he took this to be an omen signifying his own end was near. He had the branch fashioned into a coffin for himself and was buried in it in 1767. The tremendous oak he had sovenerated was mostly destroyed by fire in 1805.

One of the most enduring bits of rural weatherlore is connected with July 15, **St. Swithin's Day**,

> St. Swithin's Day, if thou dost rain,
> For forty days it will remain:
> St. Swithin's Day, if thou be fair,
> For forty days 'twill rain nae mair.

Brand's *Observations on Popular Antiquities* purports to explain the reason for this still widely popular belief. St. Swithin was a monk at Winchester Abbey in the ninth century, and a favourite of Egbert, then King of Wessex. Swithin was later promoted to Bishop of Winchester and was noteworthy both for his humility and for the great improvements he made to the city and its churches. So humble was Swithin that he made a death-bed request that he be buried not in the church, as would have been customary for a bishop, but in the north side of the churchyard, which had hitherto been relegated to the unbaptised and to suicides. He also expressed a wish that the grave night be so placed that water from the eaves would fall on it and that the parishioners would trod on it on their way to church. Although his wish was complied with on his death in 862, the order of which he was a member had a change of heart about one hundred years later and assembled to remove his remains to a more appropriate position inside Winchester Cathedral. The legend says that, on the day they were to do this, a torrential rain began and lasted for forty days, preventing the translation of his relics. They are supposed to have taken this as a sign from Heaven, warning them against the proposed action, and were instead reputed to have built a small chapel over his original and still-intact resting place.

However popular the legend is, it was disproved by Reverend Earle, a nineteenth century professor of Anglo-Saxon at Oxford University. He translated and published a tenth century Saxon manuscript, the earliest available which touches on St. Swithin. The real story is that St. Dunstan, a tenth century Archbishop of Canterbury, wanted some holy relics to be deposited in the newly rebuilt cathedral at Winchester. Dunstan was a great admirer of Swithin, as the earlier saint had also favoured a stricter monastic discipline. Moreover, Swithin had been the first to get the concession from the King of Wessex that ten percent of Royal lands would be reserved in the form of a tithe to support the Church. Swithin's popularity, combined with different reports of miraculous healings of people who prayed for intercession at his grave, resulted in King Edgar's directing that the saint's relics be removed to a shrine inside the cathedral. The early manuscript makes no mention of rain interrupting the ceremony in which the translation took place on July 15, 971.

Reverend Earle hazarded a guess that the linking of St. Swithin's Day with rain was more likely to have had its origin in pagan astrological beliefs. These might have been based on a prophecy of rain connected with prominent constellations occurring on or around July 15. With his usual thoroughness, Chambers tested the forty-day rain prophecy through the Greenwich Observatory records for the years 1640 to 1860. The test showed "that the greatest number of rainy days, after St. Swithin's Day, had taken place when the 15th of July was dry."

True or false, St. Swithin's Day's forecast is still heeded throughout the countryside. This is understandable, as it is often a time of solstitial rains, when heavy summer storms can prove devastating to the crops. Also, the farmer is impatient for sunshine during this forty day period, as that is usually critical in ensuring a successful corn harvest.

There are some stories which refer to Swithin as a drunken saint, but these are spurious, as existing records give no grounds for such allegations. These takes may have had their origins with cider makers, as Hone's *Everyday Book* points out that it was commonly held that rain on St. Swithin's Day would christen the apple crop.

St. James the Great

Another piece of June's weatherlore, connected with the 25th, **St. James's Day**, is popularized in Hertfordshire,

> Until St. James's Day is past and gone,
> There may be hops or there may be none.

The adage reminds hop growers not to count their chickens too early, especially where a crop as uncertain as hops is involved. Hope plants are extremely susceptible to blights and to the ravaging of insects.

St. James was slain by Herod around 40 AD, making him one of the first of the disciples to follow Jesus in martyrdom. James is the patron saint of Spain, as he is reputed to have been a missionary there before his death in Jerusalem. Some of his Spanish converts conveyed his body back to Spain for enshrinement, and a minor miracle occurring on that voyage is supposed to have made the scallop shell the traditional badge worn by pilgrims who pay homage to his shrine at Compostello in Galicia. In England, it used to be said that those who ate oysters on St. James's Day would never lack for money. It is likely that some of the connection of **St. James** with **oysters and scallops** has its roots in the fact that he was a fisherman before he joined the ranks of the disciples.

By the end of the month, the days have grown perceptibly shorter, and the produce of the summer's sun and rains is amply in evidence. The harvesting which has taken place during July can be seen brimming over at the greengrocers' and supermarkets. Crops such as new potatoes, peas, cauliflower, carrots, cabbages, tomatoes and radishes, which we started eating in June, are even more plentiful, and can usually be had for a better price. July adds marrows, courgettes, turnips, peppers and green beans to the table. Perhaps the most welcome addition of this month is fruit. Strawberries are a favourite, particularly if you have picked them yourself. Currants, cherries and gooseberries also come onto the market.

Cherry fairs, once popular in some counties, including Hampshire and Warwickshire, were celebrations which naturally attached themselves to cherry-picking time at the end of July. Lammastide festivities, which rejoice in the first fruits of the corn harvest, are usually associated with early August; but in the southern city of Exeter, where crops are more advanced, a **Lammas Fair** has been held on the Tuesday before the third Thursday in July.

AUGUST

***Dry August and warm
doth harvest no harm***

August used to be known as Sextilis in the old Roman calendar, meaning it was sixth month in a year which had started in March. It had only 29 days until Julius Caesar added a thirtieth. When a later Caesar, Augustus, gave the month his own name, he tacked on the thirty-first day, which was stolen from February, so that his month would not be outdone by any other in the year. Although Augustus had been born in September, he preferred to leave his namesake in the preceding month, as it had favoured him with many of the successes of his lifetime. During *Sextilis* he had first become a consul, brought three triumphs into Rome, ended a civil war and subdued Egypt.

To the Saxons August was *Arnmonath*, *Barn-Monath* and *Harvest-monath*, all references to the month's harvesting and filling of barns. The Venerable Bede claims they knew it as *Woedmonath* as well, meaning weed month, a name which has also been ascribed to their June.

In some respects August is a sad month. It is usually the last taste of real heat we have, before autumn paints the trees' leaves with their beautiful dying colours. The summer is waning, the days shorten and a few leaves have already fallen. Just before the middle of August, the swift starts its migration south, reminding us that the temperature has already begun to move towards the colder seasons which are to come. Rooks, which absented themselves overnight from their nests in the warmer weather, now begin to spend each night at home. Most of our remaining birds are relatively silent during August, though the robin red-breast begins singing again towards the end of the month.

Although most of early summer's flowers which we admired in the fields have gone, a few remain, and there are a number of new ones. The foxglove is a prominent August bloom, as is the scarlet poppy, blue harebell, the tall goldenrod and some of the daisy family. One of this month's most spectacular displays comes from the flowering heather, which transforms whole moors and hillsides to a fiery red. The pheasant's eye, which can also be seen, had a rural superstition attached to it. Unmarried country girls nicknamed it the 'rose-a-ruby', and believed that they had to have a boyfriend before it went out of flower or they would not get one until it bloomed again in the next year. But, in the cycle of the seasons, it is only right that spring's and early summer's profusions of blossoms are past. We are now entering a time set for fruition and harvest, as is attested by the thistle and dandelion seeds which fill August's air.

Fields of corn, yet to be reaped, wave in the wind like great yellow seas; a startling contrast to the still, dark hedgerows surrounding them and to the green pastureland, where cows are now enjoying the year's second crop of grass. Plums, pears and apples are ripening in the orchard trees. Old boughs of the apple trees, no longer able to bear the weight of their yield alone, are propped up with long forked crutches. Peas and beans are ready, and are usually harvested after they've become hard and dry. Not too long ago, beans were frowned up for human consumption and were thought fit to be grown for cattle only.

Hops, a climbing plant used in the making of malt liquor, begin to be harvested towards the end of August. The picking goes on through September and, in some regions, into early October. Hops are planted on little hillocks and, by the end of June or early July, have usually grown about sixteen to twenty feet up twine or poles which have been set out for them. They soon flower and then the seed vessel appears on the female plants. Once these seeds are ready, the hops are picked, dried over a charcoal fire and sold to the brewers, who use them to preserve and flavour their beer.

Of the grains, rye and oats are first to ripen. Every sunny day is valuable, as ripened corn may shed its seed, be damaged by storms or be consumed by the birds. Fortunately, summer has usually left enough behind for all, including the birds and other wildlife. With a good harvest approaching, there is an end to the universal anxiety concerning survival over the long winter ahead.

For several successive evenings at this time, we can enjoy the splendour of the harvest moon. This crimson globe appears above the horizon soon after sunset. It can make a particularly strong impression if its ascent is seen through a stand of trees or as it comes over the brow of a solitary hill.

The tiny harvest mouse also makes its appearance. It is more conspicuous now from its custom of weaving its nest up in the air, usually on several adjoining stalks of the now nearly ripe wheat, but also sometimes suspended from thistles, beanstalks or other taller plants. This curious nest, which moves to and fro in the wind, is shaped so uniformly like a ball that it is difficult to find the entrance to it. One of this animal's endearing habits is to hang by its tail from virtually anything above ground, and swing backwards and forwards for several minutes before falling asleep.

August 1 is **Lammas Day**, honouring the first fruits of the harvest. Scotland recognises it as a Quarter Day. In England it is known as a cross-Quarter Day, lying as it does half-way between Midsummer and Michaelmas. Half of the year's rent still comes due on this day in some English counties.

The most probable origin of the word Lammas, supported by the *Oxford English Dictionary,* is a shortening of the Anglo-Saxon *Hlafmaesse,* meaning Loaf-mass, an offering of loaves of bread made from the first of the new wheat. Our word 'lady' has the same root in their *hlaf-dig*, the dispenser of loaves.

Another less acceptable explanation regarding the etymology of Lammas is Lamb-mass, coming from the practice on this day of an offering of a lamb at a cathedral in York by those tenants who held its land. York Cathedral is dedicated to St Peter ad Vincula, whose feast day this is. The 'ad Vincula' means 'in chains', and is a reference to Peter's miraculous escape, recounted in the twelfth chapter of *Acts*, from the chains Herod had him bound in. Because this is **St. Peter's Day, Peter's-pence** used to become payable. It was a penny tax levied on each hearth or chimney in England, said to have been instituted by Ina, King of Wessex in 727. Pennies thus collected went to help support a school for the Angles in Rome, which would instruct and keep alive the true Roman Catholic faith in the English kings, priests and laity.

But even before Christianity came to England, the Celts celebrated the first of August as ***Lugnasad***, the third of the four festivals in their pastoral calendar. *Lugh* was the name of their sun god and *nasad* meant a gathering, in this case for festive purposes. For them, it probably honoured Lugh and marked an end of the summer shearing. It also meant the sheep could begin grazing on the stubble left in those fields which had already been harvested. Lammas-tide **sheep fairs** were once popular throughout the country, and large quantities of these animals changed hands at them.

The custom of giving thanks for the first fruits is extremely ancient. After the exodus from Egypt, Moses, in the 26th chapter of *Deuteronomy*, admonished his people to give in offering "the first of all the fruit of the earth", saying, "And now, behold, I have brought the firstfruits of the land, which thou, O Lord hast given me."

The consecration of the loaves in the Lammas service seems to have been observed solely from a religious standpoint by the Anglo-Saxons. Apparently, it never had the boisterous and festive air of a May Day about it for our medieval ancestors. Being an Anglo-Saxon practice, it is probable there was a decline in the Lammas celebrations after the Norman Conquest. At the time of the Reformation, it was deemed idolatrous, and disappeared altogether, along with many other similar customs. More than 400 years later, the Church of England finally began a revival of this and of selected other religious customs through which our forbears had honoured the natural cycle of the farming year.

Beginning in the 1940s, different parishes, mostly in southern counties, began to celebrate a **Lammas service** in the first Sunday in August. Canon Andrew Young, a winner of the Queen's Gold Medal for Poetry, was commissioned by Dr. Bell, Bishop of Chichester, to write a hymn for Lammas which appeared in the hymn book the BBC issued. It begins, "Lord, by whose breath all souls and seeds are living..."

The 1945 Lammastide issue of *The Plough*, the journal of the West

Sussex Church and Countryside Association, described the sense and sentiments with which the Lammas service should be celebrated. Although it was, in some respects, a thanksgiving, it was to be seen more as an offering, "irrespective of what the results have been or are to be." To the service, the farming community of the parish bring a loaf of bread made from the wheat which has only just ripened locally. A sheaf of wheat is also brought in and, according to Laurence Whistler in his poetically beautiful *The English Festivals*, the service sometimes starts in a field where the sheaf is cut and finishes later in the church. Appropriately enough, the participants in the service are made up of those who are most directly connected with the harvest and its fruits: a farm labourer presents the sheaf and a baker offers the loaf.

A further feature concerning the newly resurrected Lammas service is that, in some churches, the loaf of first fruits which is offered at the altar is subsequently employed as the Communion wafer. During the Exeter Lammas fair, which was celebrated in late July, farmers had the custom of breaking a Lammas loaf and scattering it in the corners of their barns, sanctifying their storehouse which soon would be bulging with the rest of the fruits of the harvest.

August 5 is the feast day of **St. Oswald**, who was **King of Northumbria** in the seventh century. The church at Guiseley, Yorkshire, which is dedicated to St. Oswald, is clipped on this day. **'Clipping the Church'** is a very old custom in which the parishioners join hands and move in a circle around their church, affirming their religion through this physical 'embrace' with it. On the Saturday nearest St. Oswald's Day **rushes** are **strewn** in the church at Grasmere, Cumbria, although the floor of this building has been boarded since 1841.

An early August custom nostalgic of the Middle Ages is the **Grand Wardmote** meeting of the Woodmen of Arden at the village of Meriden in Warwickshire. The Woodmen are a company of archers, limited in number to eighty, who enjoy archery competitions at this meet. In accordance with medieval standards, they use six-foot yew bows to shoot their arrows.

An August saying reminds us of the end of summer and of the chilly air begun to be felt in the evenings towards the end of this month:

St. Bartholomew
Brings the dew.

August 24 is **St. Bartholomew's Day**. He was one of the Apostles and is mentioned in the first three Gospels. Little is known about his history after his appearance in the upper room in the first chapter of *Acts*. Legend has it that, while on a mission to Armenia, he was martyred by being flayed alive. This story has led to a knife becoming his emblem. St. Bartholomew is said to bless the mead made by a group of monks in Cornwall, and one of his many roles is consequently that of patron saint to makers of honey.

Bartholomew fairs used to be extremely popular at a number of centres in England. At more rural locations and market towns, farmers could sell surplus horses, cattle and sheep they did not feel it prudent to keep through another winter. The most famous and undoubtedly longest continuing Bartholomew Fair was the one held at Smithfield in London. It was started by a man named Rahere who had been minstrel and jester to Henry I. He claimed to have seen St. Bartholomew in a vision, and to have been directed to found, in the Saint's honour, a hospital and church at Smithfield. A monastery was built in 1123, after Henry II granted the land to him, along with the right to hold a three day fair. At first, the fair had both it temporal and spiritual sides. Merchants would sell cattle and goods, while pilgrims attended a church festival.

LEE AND HARPER'S BOOTH, BARTHOLOMEW FAIR.   FAUX THE CONJUROR'S BOOTH.

Actors and Conjuror's Booths, Bartholomew Fair

However, as the centuries passed, the temporal side gained an ascendency which eventually eclipsed the spiritual. By the time Ben Jonson wrote his comedy on the fair in 1614, those who participated in it came strictly for amusement. Under Charles II, after the Restoration, the fair was extended to fourteen days, and it was such a well-attended event that the city's theatres closed during it, and their actors performed instead on booths at the fair.

Pepys' diaries mention visits to the Bartholomew Fair in 1667 and 1668. The riotous crowds and carnival-like atmosphere of the proceedings led, in 1708, to its being reduced back to its original three days. One of the last good descriptions available of the fair as it used to be is given by Hone, who visited it in 1822. Much of the emphasis of his write-up concerns the various freaks, each of whom could be seen for a price. The fair was increasingly suppressed by civic authorities and finally discontinued in 1855, 732 years after it had first started.

Although Bartholomew Fairs have died out, there is one celebration in his honour which still takes place at the Yorkshire village of West Witton, where the parish church is dedicated to him. On a Saturday near August 24, a figure called the **Bartle** is paraded through the village and then **burnt** on a large bonfire. Although it is now confined to one day, the celebration used to take place on St. Bartholomew's Day itself, and heralded the beginning of a week-long festival. There are different theories concerning the Bartle's original identity. Christina Hole suggests he may have represented a pre-Christian harvest diety who later gained his name from the coincidence of the sacrificial ceremony with the feast day of their parish church's patron saint.

August, with its harvest filling the barn, usually gave assurances that households would not go hungry during the winter. But this was not always the case. Records of famine are not infrequent in our history books and, all too often, they were followed by plague. The worst was undoubtedly the dreaded Black Death of 1348-9, which occurred after the 1348 harvest could not be taken in due to continuous rains and flooding. Whole villages perished, and it is estimated that a third of the population of England died.

The last significant outbreak of epidemic was the Great Plague in 1665, which killed 68,000 Londoners. Although it was mostly confined to the capital, other more rural villages also suffered from it, and in one, Eyam in Derbyshire, a plague memorial service is still held on the last Sunday in August. The epidemic was introduced in Eyam in August 1665, through some cloth which had been sent from London to a local tailor. When the disease began spreading through the town, William Mompesson, Eyam's Rector, asked his parishioners not to flee, for fear of communicating the contagion to the neighbouring towns and countryside. Although it meant risking their lives, the villagers agreed and remained in Eyam while the plague ran its course for the next thirteen months. Mompesson had closed the church, but continued to hold services in the open air at a place called Cucklett Delf. Out of an original population of 350, only 91 of Eyam's villagers lived to see the autumn of 1666; but, through their heroism, they were largely successful in preventing further outbreaks in the neighbourhood. The **plague memorial service** for those who perished still takes place, and is held, appropriately enough, in the open air of Cucklett Delf.

Before the combine-harvester came into virtual universal use, it was a common sight to see the fields alive with workers harvesting corn throughout August and into September. The harvest often took up to six weeks on a good-sized farm. The process started with the sharp sickles in the field, and ended with the careful thatching of ricks, with many steps between the two. The labourers enjoyed ale from wooden flagons while they worked, and the pubs were filled with thirsty reapers in the evenings.

To our modern urban dweller, August is synonymous with a holiday by the seaside or a package tour abroad, but to the farmer, ancient and modern, August is probably the busiest month of the year.

Plenty of the harvest is in evidence on the table, with July's offerings still available as well as some new items: field mushrooms, cucumbers, swedes, celery and summer beans. Of fruit, tomatoes are probably at their most plentiful, and supplies of plums and of cooking and eating apples begin to be abundant.

SEPTEMBER

September blow soft
Till the fruits are in the loft

This month's name derives from its having had seventh place in the Roman year. With Julius Caesar's reformation of the calendar, September was given a thirty-first day, but this was later taken away by Augustus. Except for a very short period, this month has remained unchanged since that time. The short exception occurred during the reign of Domitian, a tyrant who assumed the title Germanicus. He considered it appropriate that September bear his title, and that the next month, October, be called by his family name. Soon after he had effected these changes, he was murdered, and the two months had their earlier names restored to them.

To the Anglo-Saxons, September was known as *Gerstmonath*, and sometimes as *Haligemonath*. *Gerst* to them was barley, which ripened in September, happily ensuring sufficient raw material for them to make bread and their important beverage, beer. The two words, beer and barley, are thought to come from the same root in Old English. The term *Haligemonath* meant 'holy month', for it was during September that the pagan Saxons held a celebration which combined feasting with a meting out of justice by their priests. These festivities were eventually suppressed, albeit with some difficulty, by our early Christian fathers.

September heralds the true beginning of autumn. The days have considerably shortened and, although the temperature is generally warm, a distinct chill can be felt in the morning and evening.

The birds give another key to the change in the seasons. The stone-curlew can be heard in the south and east, and the tawny, or wood-, owl begins hooting in the forests. The woodlark, blackbird and thrush are also heard. Towards the end of the month swallows take their leave of us. Not too long ago, it was theorised that they spent their winters either in a torpid state in caverns like bats, or even that they kept themselves in a similar condition under water. Their migration south, like that of many other of our birds of passage, has since been observed and recorded.

A few members of the thrush family, including the redwing and fieldfare, begin arriving in England after summers spent in countries even further north than ours. They will pass the winter enjoying the berries and fruit which have ripened in the woods and hedgerows before flying north again in the spring.

Before the days of conservation and the general outcry against hunting, September was recognised as the beginning of the shooting season of the partridge and black-grouse, though the season for other of the grouse family had started towards the end of August. The timings of these hunting seasons were, no doubt, originally based on the life-cycles of the birds and on their readiness for the table. Chambers quotes some other reasons for the timing of this pastime enjoyed by the wealthier classes, taken from an article on 'Shooting' which appeared in the *Encyclopedia Britannica* well over one hundred years ago:

> Many circumstances contribute to the popularity of grouse-shooting;   among which may be enumerated the following. It commences during the   parliamentary recess and long vacation --- the legislator's, lawyer's and   collegian's holiday; and it is no wonder that, after having been cooped up   all the summer, these or any other classes of society should seek   relaxation in the sports of the field... It is the season when every one, from the peer to the shopkeeper, who can afford the indulgence, either   rusticates or travels. In that month the casual tourist, the laker, and the
> angler are often in the north, where the temptation to draw a trigger is   irresistible.

But another writer of the same period, quoted by Howitt from Chronicle of the Seasons, seems to have foreseen, in a modified form, some of today's conservationist's viewpoint concerning such field sports:

> "In the zeal for destruction which seems to pervade all ranks and classes of society at this particular period, it may seem out of place to speak of the usefulness of the animals which form the special object of the pursuit, or to offer a recommendation in

their behalf, that the war against the species may be regulated and kept within due bounds, so that man may not reduce their numbers to his own injury. In the case of the partridge, as well as that of many other birds, it is fully believed that if we understand their habits aright, we should often be disposed to cherish that which we are now so zealous to destroy."

Through its evolution, the partridge has built up a particularly compassionate, almost human, method of defending itself against sportsmen, or other creatures of prey, when its brood is too young to fly. If in danger in these circumstances, the two parent birds fly off, while the young remain motionless and hidden in the plant growth. The cock flies only a short distance, lands and then appears to try to struggle away, dragging its wings behind it. Sensing an easy kill from this diversion, it is usually followed by the hunter or his pointer, and thus is able to lead them away from its young. The hen, however, has meanwhile landed a few hundred yards away and, hidden by the undergrowth, rushes back on ground to her brood, which she then leads to safety. If the male has managed to escape, he hears their calls and rejoins his family in their new hiding place. If the cock is not with the family when danger approaches, the hen acts out his part to draw the pursuit away from her offspring.

September also brings a wintry rendezvous of herring in the Arctic Circle. They stay there until the spring, when they move south to spawn in warmer climes, providing fresh seafood for fishermen in the English Channel and Irish Sea.

Although September is a month of harvest rather than of flowers, there are a few blooms, including those of the ivy and of the wild thyme. In the Essex countryside, the saffron is an important flowering plant. Saffron Walden, near Cambridge, has been the centre for this harvest. The saffron flowers for about three weeks during this month, and the blossoms are gathered just before they open completely. The parts of the flower which are used act as a colourful yellow dye in cooking, and were once thought to be helpful as a medicinal cordial. Saffron is an understandably expensive product to buy as, from a whole acre, one is lucky to reap ten pounds of product.

Seeds from the summer's blossoms fly through the air, while

orchards and hedgerows are decorated with their colourful fruit.
Hawthorn berries turn red and bramble ones black. Hips form where
wild roses bloomed only last month. Different fruits, including the
sloe and the crab apple begin to ripen.

The first day of September is dedicated to **St. Giles**. As he is the
patron saint of many parish churches, his feast day gave rise to
festivals being celebrated in the villages with churches named for
him. This seventh century saint is thought to have been Greek by
birth. However, not finding sufficient solitude in his homeland, he is
supposed to have sailed to Marseilles and then to have made his way
north until he found an isolated spot in a forest. Here he lived as a
hermit, gaining part of his daily sustenance from the milk of a hind.
One day, the royal hunt, in pursuit of this very hind, shot an arrow at it
which Giles is said to have caught in his hand in mid-flight. The King,
upon hearing of this deed, was so impressed he offered Giles land for
a monastery.

Another legend has it that Giles was crippled in one leg, and that he
refused to be cured on the grounds that lameness would aid him in
mortifying the flesh. As a consequence, he has become the patron
saint of cripples, lepers and beggars. London's St. Giles,
Cripplegate, is one of the notable examples of the churches named
after him.

A **St. Giles Fair** is still held annually in Oxford on the first two
weekdays following the first Sunday after September 1. The fair is
mainly comprised of vending stalls set up in the streets bordering St.
Giles' Church, but has little in common with the original celebration.
That started as a wake, or vigil, at the church which was observed by
parishioners on St. Giles' Eve. Gradually, though, a secular holiday
was added and a variety of goods began to be sold in the streets
around the church and, by the sixteenth century, it had become more
famous as a fair and festival than for its original religious purpose.

September 1 is also the grand opening of the **oyster season** in
Essex. This dates from a charter granted to the town of Colchester in
1186 by Richard I. Colchester's Mayor ceremonially harvests the first
oysters from a boat, after a proclamation dating from the thirteenth

century is read by a clerk to him and others from the town council.

The Monday after the first Sunday following September 4 is the first day of the Abbots Bromley Wakes Week, and an ancient **Horn Dance** is performed in this Staffordshire town. A Wakes Week, again deviating from its original purpose as a night spent awake at a parish church on the eve of its patron saint's feast day, became more commonly known in industrial towns as an annual holiday week occurring when their local factories had their shutdown. The Horn Dance celebrated at Abbots Bromley is extremely old and, according to some sources, is thought to be representative of one of the most primitive dances extant in Europe. One of the earliest references to it, Robert Plot's *Natural History of Staffordshire*, was published in 1686. At that time the dance was considered to have been celebrated on December 25, January 1 and again on Twelfth Day. The implication from these dates is that it originally had to do with a fertility rite connected with the winter solstice's rebirth of the sun. The facts that reindeer horns are worn during it, and that local legend claims the dance celebrates ancient village hunting rights in nearby Needwood Forest, suggest that this custom's roots pre-date the arrival of Christianity in England.

The six pairs of horns worn during the ceremony are mounted on wooden replicas of deer-heads. Three of them are painted blue and the other three white. Their spans vary from twenty-nine to thirty-nine inches, and their origins are unknown. Christina Hole suggests in *A Dictionary of British Folk Customs* that, if they were British in origin, they should date back to the twelfth century, the period when British reindeer are thought to have become extinct. Another theory is that the horns are more recent spoils of a Scandinavian settler in this district, who had brought them as a nostalgic memento of his homeland.

The dance at Abbots Bromley includes twelve participants. Six of them wear the white and blue horns, while the other six seem to be a combination of some of the actors of the May Day Mummers Pageant. These, in costume, are said to represent a Fool, a man dressed as Maid Marian, a Bowman, a Hobby Horse and an accordion-player. In a manner somewhat reminiscent of Rogationtide

practices, the dancers make a twenty-mile walk around the Abbots
Bromley parish, stopping to do their dance outside of the houses on
their way. If the ceremony is omitted at any house, it is supposed to
be a sign of bad luck for its occupants.

September 14 used to commonly be known as **Holy Rood Day**. A
rood is a crucifix, or Christ's cross. Rood-screens and rood-lofts,
which are representations of the cross, separating the nave from the
choir in many churches, are derived from the word rood. Many early
English churches were named after the Holy Rood. And, during the
Middle Ages, the 14th was an important feast day.

Because this day coincides with the ripening of the hazel-nut, it used
to be customary for groups to go **nutting** in the woods on Holy Rood
Day. A basket of nuts was a tribute a gallant beau often paid his
favourite girl. In the case of prettier maidens, several baskets would
be received, each from a different hopeful suitor. Presumably, the
disappearance of woods in England has contributed to the decline in
nutting practices.

Another nut, the acorn, begins to be shed by the oak around this
time. Acorns are thought to have once been one of the chief foods of
primitive man, and latterly became a favourite seasonal food for
swine.

"Clipping the Church", as was celebrated in Guiseley, Yorkshire, on
August 5 is also performed, but in September, at St. Mary's Church in
Painswick, Glaucestershire. The date chosen is the Sunday nearest
the feast day of the Nativity of Our Lady. As they use the date
according to the Old Julian calendar, this makes it the Sunday closest
to September 19. After a procession of children approach the church
and surround it holding hands, they perform the Clipping ceremony in
the older traditional style by moving in towards the church and then
back away from it three times. Although this once more widely
spread chustom is considered to have originally been a rite
welcoming spring, in those parishes where it is still practiced, it often
now occurs on or near the local patron saint's day. A nineteenth

century writer on the Painswick Clipping festival drew parallels which suggested it had its roots in the Roman *Lupercalia*, a pagan ritual of spring which was celebrated on February 15.

September 21 is **St. Matthew's Day**. Matthew was author of the first of the books of the *New Testament*, and his literacy may have been a by-product of his unenviable profession of tax-gathering, which preceded his discipleship. After the crucifixion, Matthew is thought to have preached in Judea and then in Ethiopia, where he was martyred after rebuking the local king for desiring a young maiden who had made her vows of virginity.

As this date is significant in approximately marking the autumnal equinox, when the length of the night starts becoming longer than that of the day, the saying arose,

> *Saint Matthew, get candlesticks new,*
> *Saint Matthi, lay candlesticks by.*

St. "Matthi". Or Matthias', Day, it will be remembered, is February 24, when the days are once again lengthening, and less candlelight would accordingly be needed.

Although apple crops can ripen anytime between July and October, depending on their variety and the latitude where they are grown, the largest proportion of their harvest usually occurs in September. The taking in of this crop permits a start-up of the cider-making process, notably in the counties of Devon, Somerset and Worcester. The apples are set by for a short period to mature before being crushed and pressed to extract their juice. The transformation is completed by fermenting the product. Farmhouse scrumpy is a very tasty, though more rustic, version, usually only available in its best form at or near apple growing districts. Some of the pear crop, which also comes in at this time, is treated in a similar manner to make perry.

The corn harvest, which began in August in the south, is usually completed in the Midlands and in the north sometime during

September. This activity used to be one of the most colourful and impressive sights of the year. The fields would be dotted with industrious men and women felling the waving yellow sea of corn with sickles. An accomplished reaper could fell an armful with a single swipe. A helper would follow him, putting a band around each sheaf and standing eight to ten sheaves up together to make a stook. Gleaners, usually children, came after with bags and scissors. They would collect any corn which had been missed and, after cutting off these stalks, put the ears into their bags. Gleanings used to form an important part of winter stores in most rural homes. The tradition goes back at least to the Old Testament, where Ruth is described as meeting her husband Boaz while gleaning in his fields. After the stooks had been forked onto the wagons, the richest gleanings would always be found where they had stood.

A manual corn harvest often took from four to six weeks to complete. Everyone involved would watch out for the last wagonload to be taken to the rick-yard, and often the labourers would join in in a great Harvest Shout, which could be heard for miles around. The words shouted varied from region to region, but their purpose was partly friendly competition, to advise the neighbouring farmers that one had one's crop in, and partly an expression of relief that there would be food for the coming months. Birds and field mice perform the final gleanings, collecting the ears of corn both from the fields and from the wagon droppings.

The most common form of Harvest Shout was that of **"Crying the Mare"** (or the Neck). When the last stalks of corn in the field were gathered together to the cut, an appointed labourer, called the Harvest Lord, would raise them in the air and cry out "I have her! I have her! I have her!" His fellow workers, whose task was now complete, would ask, "What hast thee? What hast thee? What hast thee?" His response would be "A mare! A mare! A mare!" This was sometimes followed by the further question of "Whose is her? Whose is her? Whose is her?" to which the answer was the thrice repeated name of the farmer whose crop had now been gathered. To the final question of "Where shall we send her?" the Harvest Lord would name an adjoining farmer who was still reaping. Although the words varied from county to county, the emotion expressed was the same, a relieved thanksgiving that the crop was in.

This last sheaf to be cut was formed into a **Corn Dolly**, or **Kern Baby**, and was thought to have been the final refuge of the Corn Spirit in the field. As it would have been most unwise for any man to sever the field's connection with this benevolent god, it became a bit of a challenge as to who would cut it. At some locations, it was arranged that several of the labourers would stand around the last sheaf and throw their sickles at it. With this practice, it was usually impossible to determine whose sickle had made the final cut. But, in some districts, if observers had noted the man who had delivered the telling blow, he would receive a good deal of humorous physical abuse from his fellow workers. According to Christina Hole, this sort of treatment might well have had its origins in pre-Christian rites which called for the sacrifice of the reaper who had felled the last of the corn. This theory finds ample support in early Egyptian practice, where it was thought that the completion of a harvest meant an end to their god Osiris. In the 21st chapter of *II Samuel*, there is an account of human sacrifices being made to put an end to three years of famine.

The Corn Dolly is fashioned into a variety of shapes by weaving a number of stalks together. When the dolly is made in a human form, the ears of corn represent the head, and are sometimes also used for hands and feet. Since it symbolised the goddess or spirit of the crop, it would be taken to the Harvest Home feast, after which it was reverently placed by the farmer's hearth. Later, on Plough Monday in January, it was returned to the earth in the first furrow to vouchsafe that next year's harvest would also be plentiful.

The **Harvest Home** was a celebration supper provided by the farmer for all who had participated in the harvest. It followed the last load, known as the **Hock Cart**, to come in from the fields. For this load, the wagon, decorated with branches and flowers, would carry singing and shouting workers and, sometimes, a figure made from a standing sheaf and a **Harvest Queen**. The Queen would be decked out with a straw hat into which had been woven flowers and ears of corn.

Those accompanying the Hock Cart often sang a traditional song commemorating the event. The songs varied by district, but this version gives a representative idea of their sentiments,

Harvest Home

The fare at Harvest Home could be counted on to be generous, and its consumption to be accompanied by plenty of good ale, songs and toasts. Such feasts were sanctioned by Moses in *Deuteronomy*, chapter 16:

<blockquote>

"Thou shalt observe the feast of tabernacles seven days, after that thou hast gathered in thy corn and thy wine: And thou shalt rejoice in thy feast, thou, and thy son, and thy daughter, and thy manservant, and thy maidservant, and the Levite, and the stranger, the fatherless and the widow that are within thy gates."

</blockquote>

Although some farmers still keep up the tradition of the Harvest Home, it has in the main fallen victim to the combine harvester and the consequent need for only comparatively few workers to take up a very large crop. The author had only seen tantalising photographs and etchings of the traditional harvest until he made a trip to the Scottish Isle of Raasay in the Inner Hebrides in September, 1981, where he was able to observe two elderly men reaping a field of corn with sickles in the old manner. He would like to think the Harvest Home found a refuge in their thanksgiving after their small crop was completely taken in.

The difference in the labour involved in the new and old ways in astonishing. J.H.B. Peel, in his "Country Talks" column in *The Daily Telegraph*, mentioned having seen 200 acres of corn harvested in one day by a machine and three men, whereas an account of the harvesting of a similar acreage in 1389 reveals that it took 520 men two days. The first reaping machine, invented by Rev. Patrick Bell in 1826, was not manufactured commercially until 1853. Even then it was very slow in finding favour with the farmers. The ones who did buy it often found it broken up by their labourers, who had the real concern that the machine would result in the loss of their jobs. One is half inclined to agree with the workers. The very significant advantages brought about by today's agricultural mechanisation is counterbalanced by an equally really loss of tradition. Not only have we sacrificed the communal sharing of the suffering and joy in the harvest, the thrift the young learned from gleaning and the celebration of the Harvest Home, but we may soon come to a time when the country's youth will not know what an ear of corn looks like, though they eat and drink the products made from it every day.

In spite of the decline of the Harvest Home, **Harvest Thanksgiving services** are now held at many churches throughout England. The revival began with the eccentric Rev. Hawker, at Morwenstow, Cornwall, in 1843, who invited his parishioners to attend a Sacrament "in the bread of the new corn." Anglican Harvest Thanksgivings are usually timed for late September or early October.

Part of the importance of **Michaelmas Day** on September 29 is due to a Christianising of the earlier pagan agricultural celebrations having to do with the autumnal equinox. The Church teaches that, like St. Gabriel and St. Raphael, St. Michael is an archangel. The five references to Michael in the Bible, beginning in *Daniel*, all ascribe a warlike character to him. In *Revelations*, Michael is credited with leading the loyal angels in the battle which resulted in Satan and his crew being cast out of heaven. The feast day of St. Michael and All Angels on the 29th is a reminder to Christian worshippers of the powers angels have to intercede on man's behalf. The first church dedicated to St. Michael was built near Constantinople during the fourth century and, soon after that, Pope Boniface erected a basilica in his honour on the site of Circus Maximus in Rome.

In England, Michaelmas is a quarter day, when rents became due. Tenants were often provided a feast by their landlords. Traditional Michaelmas fare is goose, a practice dating at least as far back as the reign of Edward IV (1461-1483), when records indicate that the rent payment required from one man was in the form of "one goose fit for the Lord's dinner." Geese are at their finest at this time, having fattened themselves on the stubble left in the fields after the harvest. There is a story that Queen Elizabeth I was enjoying her **Michaelmas goose** when the news of the defeat of the Spanish Armada was brought to her. A superstition gradually arose that eating a goose on Michaelmas brought luck. Chambers quotes a dialogue locking this which appeared in 1709 in British Apollo:

> "Q. - *Yet my wife would persuade me (as I am a sinner)*
> *To have a fat goose for St. Michael dinner:*
> *And then all the year round, I pray you would mind it,*
> *I shall not want money —oh, grant I may find it!*

Now several there are that believe this is true,
Yet the reason of this is desired from you."

"A. - We think you're so far from the having of more,
That the price of the goose you have less than before
The custom came up from the tenants presenting
Their landlords with geese to incline their relenting
On following payments..."

Many agricultural fairs used to be held on Michaelmas Day, and a good number of them were observed on or near October 10, its dating by the Old Style. In addition to the sale of cattle, sheep and geese, many of them were known as **"Hiring Fairs"**. Since the agricultural year comes to a close with the harvest, contracts for farm labourers were often dated from one Michaelmas to the next. These workers, both male and female, accordingly released from their prior year's contracts, would assemble at the fair, wearing or carrying a badge of their trade, in hopes of obtaining a contract for the new year.

Tenancies for many farms are still dated to expire on Michaelmas, and advertisements offering farmlands would be placed around this date.

Another custom which used to be practiced in different parish churches on St. **Michael's Eve**, September 28, was that of **nut-cracking**, reminiscent in some respects to the Wakes traditions.

In light of Michaelmas being the punctuation point to one agricultural year and the commencement of a new one, various weatherlore sayings arose. One of these is,

A dark Michaelmas,
And a light Christmas.

meaning that a sunny winter was to follow a cloudy or wet September 29. Another old saw seems to cancel this one out:

"If Michaelmas Day be fair, the sun will shine much in the winter: though the wind in the north-east will frequently reign long, and be very sharp and nipping."

As for so many of our weatherlore sayings, the meteorologist Paul Marriot has checked these out and published his findings in his book *Red Sky at Night Shepherd's Delight?* For the years that he has sampled, both of the above sayings proved to be the exception rather than the rule.

Towards the end of September, as is appropriate now that we have entered autumn, the leaves on our trees are turning brown in earnest. With the harvest in, the farmers begin ploughing their fields for winter corn, rye and wheat, which are sown either in this month or the next. Potatoes are lifted and, as befits the season, jams and jellies are made. As September is the harvest month, the table sees more local produce, including runner beans, carrots, celery, beetroot, cabbages and onions, as well as peppers, shallots, tomatoes, turnips and parsnips. Different varieties of apples are plentiful. Although strawberries are waning, cobnuts, blackberries, plums and pomegranates help to complete the dinner.

OCTOBER

In October dung your field
And your land its wealth will yield

Our name for this month derives from its having been the eighth in the old Latin calendar. The Saxons knew October as *Wymonat*, or wine-month, as during this month wine was available either from local production or from nearby countries. This would have been truer of Saxons in Germany than of those in England, as earlier English inhabitants were more accustomed to imbibing their locally produced beer, cider and mead. It was also known as *Winter-fyllith*, supposedly from October's full moon being reckoned by them to mark the approach of winter.

With October's entrance, any remaining fanciful hopes of an eternal summer are inexorably brought to an end. Herbaceous plants die down to their roots. Leaves yellow and drop from the trees. Seeds are scattered to distant parts by the wind and, unwittingly, by animals and birds. The sun itself seems to have forsaken us for more southerly climes. Yet, in spite of the decay all around, reminding us of our own inevitable and approaching end, there is a scenic beauty to autumn which is reminiscent in its own way to that of spring. The fading leaves on shrubbery and trees give a richness of colour to the countryside that could never be appreciated when those same leaves began to form. And, as they fall, we find their absence opens up new vistas of distant country which had lain unknown or forgotten with summer's heavy foliage.

Every gust of wind now rattles and rustles the dying leaves, showering them down on us. The walnut is one of the first to shed, followed closely by the ash and then by the lime and the poplar. Some of the richest and most beautiful varieties of autumn colour can be seen in the changing oak, beech and elm. The horse-chestnut, an immigrant to England from Greece in the early 17th century, also provides a spectacular golden sight. Although cattle and deer will eat its nuts, horses will not. Its common name mistakenly derives from a belief that it bears a variety of chestnut, as well as that it would cure horses of chest complaints, when in fact it is poisonous to them.

This death of plants can be likened symbolically in some respects to the transformation taught by the major religions for, without it, we could not count upon spring's joyous resurrection. The falling leaves are a good example of this. The reason they drop off, often before they are completely dead, is due to new buds and branches pushing out and forcing the older leaves away. These will give us the first of our new spring greenery, though they will stop growing and lie dormant during the colder intervening winter months. The tiny branches which form where these new buds start ensures a replacement by several leaves for each of the old ones lost. Evergreen trees, which now begin to seem full of extra life in comparison with their nearly naked neighbours, follow a similar law. But in their case, the new buds wait until the spring before pushing away the old needles.

October introduces a changing note in our bird life. Swallows can be seen gathering at focal points each night, and then dispersing in groups again during the daytime. Soon they fly off south to their winter homes. The house martin usually leaves its nest under the eaves by mid-October, after having raised its second brood. Rooks begin to foregather in the trees by their ancestral homes just before dusk. They seem to play at sport with each other, flying and diving through the air, before retiring to their nests at night. The partridge is one of the few birds' calls which can be heard in the first half of this month.

We begin to see some newcomers with the autumn. Different waterfowl arrive on our shores from their summer homes in the arctic. The redwing also arrives, its song enlivening a wood or meadow on a sunny day. The immigration of the fieldfare comes with some ominous weather lore attached to its timing. An early arrival is said to be a sign of a hard winter. A similar harbinger of difficult times is the old saw which guarantees a long and cold winter if there are lots of haws and berries in the bushes to feed the fieldfare and other migrants if they arrive early. But an early autumnal arrival of our birds of passage is, no doubt, more likely caused by a cooler than usual temperature in the places they've flown *from*. The hooded crow may also be seen in northern and eastern England. Cold weather and snow drive it away from its summer home in Scotland.

October is the beginning of the new year in the farming cycle. The fields are ploughed, and oats and wheat are sown. Banking, ditching and repairing of fences are gates are other agricultural chores during this month. A few of the crops are still being taken in, including potatoes, carrots, beetroot, turnips and the last of the yield from the orchards. With winter's approach, 'free' hours are spent felling trees and gathering other fuel for the cooler months. In some areas the flocks of sheep are driven into enclosures, or folds, in the evenings for protection against the chill night air.

Most of the traditional regional celebrations which occurred during the first half of October were in the nature of agricultural fairs reminiscent of those held towards the end of September. Many were grouped around Michaelmas Day, Old Style, but most of the older ones have now disappeared. Some were **Hiring, or 'Mop', Fairs**, at which male and female labourers would enter into a contract for the new agricultural year. A few weeks later, in different locations in the Midlands, the custom of the **'run-away mop'** took place. This was an opportunity for workers who were dissatisfied with their new employers to seek a more congenial one, rather than see out the year in the service of the farmer they had originally contracted with.

With October's colder nights, and on throughout the winter, travelling used to be much more hazardous than it is today. This was especially true for poorer travellers in the days before roads were both paved and signposted. Originally, religious houses and monastic communities helped to provide food and a resting place for those who were lost or too poor to find anything else. Later, private individuals began leaving bequests which were to be used for similar purposes. One form of this assistance which developed in a number of communities was a **'Lost in the Dark Bell'**, which would be rung each evening through the colder months, when dusk fell earlier, to help lost travellers find their way back to habitation. Up until 1939 in Charlton-on-Otmoor, Oxfordshire, a bell of this sort was rung from the 11th of October until Lady Day. One rider who was saved by hearing a similar bell at Twyford, in Hampshire, bequeathed an **annual dinner** to Twyford's **bellringers**, which is held each October 7, the anniversary of the date on which the sound of the bell rescued him.

October 18 is **St. Luke's Day**. Although Luke was the author of the third Gospel and of the Acts of the Apostles, very little is known of his life. He is believed to have come from Antioch and, from a verse in the last chapter of *Colossians*, to have trained as a physician. He joined St. Paul about 50 AD, and was later with Paul in Rome when the latter was imprisoned there. While nothing is known for sure about his last days and death, Jerome has written that Luke's bones were translated to Constantinople in 357. Since Luke is such a prominent saint and apostle, and because his feast day occurs in mid-October, the period around the 18th became popularised as 'St. Luke's Little Summer'. The warmish and sunny days, or Indian summer, which sometimes *does* occur around this time also gave rise to the couplet,

> *On St. Luke's Day*
> *The oxen have leave to play.*

An identical saying, with about the same chance of being correct, has also been applied to **St. Jude's Day**, October 28.

St. Crispin's Day, on the 25th, should more properly be known as **Crispin's and Crispinian's Day**, for they were brothers who were martyred together in northern France. Roman by origin, but coming to France as missionaries, they earned their living as cobblers, following the example of St. Paul, who made tents rather than be a burden to any other man. After their martyrdoms in the third century, a legend has it their bodies were cast into the sea to be washed up later in the environs of the Romney Marsh in Kent.

The famous battle of Agincourt, which took place on October 25, 1415, was memorable enough to be celebrated in England for several centuries afterwards, and consequently lent some patriotic fervour to the feast day of Crispin and Crispinian. In Shakespeare's *Henry the Fifth*, the English monarch who led the attack, some impetus is added to the association between the saints's day and the battle through Henry being given the words in this drama: "And Crispin Crispian shall ne'er go by ... but we in it shall be remembered." The fact that Henry's forces were said to have been outnumbered six to one gives even more reason to celebrate this particular victory.

Because of their trade, Crispin and Crispinian naturally became patron saints of shoemakers. Members of that craft throughout England used to celebrate their feast day with processions, a holiday and merrymaking. Up until well into the nineteenth century, a few parishes celebrated the day by hanging up an effigy of the saint at a public place on Crispin's Eve. The next day it was cut down and carried in a procession through the town, while its garments were distributed to the local members of the shoemakers' guild. What was left of the effigy was rolled into a ball of sorts and kicked around the crowd before being burnt.

October 31 is the first of two days set aside for the Vigil and Feast of All Saints. It is better known as **All Hallows Eve**, which has long since been shortened to Hallowe'en, and since further simplified to Halloween. A Christian Feast of All Saints has been observed since as early as the seventh century. The date for its celebration changed from May13 to November 1 in 835. All Soul's Day, on November 2, was instituted by the Abbot of Cluny in France, probably in about 1030, allowing us the short space of two days to honour and remember *all* of the dead, saints and sinners alike. The name Hallowtide attached itself to the three days running from October 31 to November 2.

The belief, during this season, that the ominous door separating this world from the next one is open is much more ancient than these Christian practices. With the fields ploughed and the principle crops just sown, this period was also significant in being the start of the new farming year. As such, many superstitions attached themselves to this time of beginnings, and a great variety of divinations were performed in an effort to learn what the outcome of the year would be.

November 1 was the Eve of the Celtic winter, a dreaded season which would extend until the following May Day. They knew the day as *Samhain*, the last of their pastoral year's quarter days. For them, it meant rounding up their flocks; to better protect those that would be kept through the winter, and to slaughter all others for which there would not be enough food. They enjoyed a Festival of Fire at dusk on neighbouring hilltops, similar to those which had been lit for the dying sun on Midsummer's Eve, and danced around and through these fires as a means of protecting themselves against evil spirits, as well as for purification for the new year.

All Hallows Eve bonfires were still popular throughout England up until the nineteenth century, partly as a safeguard against witches, but also as a ceremonial rite for the relief of the souls of those who had passed on but were still in purgatory.

The continuity of the Celtic *Samhain* Fire Fesitval is so remarkable as almost to indicate an inborn instinct for this celebration at this time of year. The custom survived the Christianisation of England, the Norman Conquest, the Reformation and the succeeding growth of the Puritans. Birds migrate, lemmings drop voluntarily to their deaths in the sea and other mammals hibernate. Human beings light bonfires to mark the beginning of November. The custom *still* survives today, only it has been moved five days forward, closer to the date the Celtic people used for their *Samhain*, which would have been November 12 in the Old Style. Our instinct to light fires at this time of year, however, is now rationalised as an occasion for honouring Guy Fawkes' Day.

The earliest annual celebrations of Halloween customs occur in the West Country, particularly in Devon and Somerset. These are held on the last Thursday in October. The one enjoyed at Hinton St. George in Somerset is probably the most renown. There, a **procession of children carry lanterns** made of hollowed out and intricately decorated pumpkins, with candles alight inside. They are led by an appointed Punkie King and Queen, and make their rounds of the villagers' houses, singing a verse at each and asking for a candle and a light. Invariably, though, they had already begged their candles from neighbours before the procession began.

An interesting local legend tries to explain the roots of this practice. It seems that, long ago, some of the male villagers were off to the nearby Chiselborough Fair which, coincidentally, used to be held on the last Thursday in October. Having had too much to drink, they were understandably later than usual in arriving home. The anxious wives, concerned at their non-appearance, are said to have made lanterns from mangolds, and to have begged candles and money from other villagers so that they could set off in search of the missing men ...and a similar procession is supposed to have been held at the village on the anniversary of this occasion ever since.

In fact, **lantern-bearing processions** were popular on Halloween throughout the country. The lanterns were made from turnips, swedes or pumpkins, which had alarming faces carved on them, and through which the candle-light shone. These were held up on poles to present a frightening illuminated aspect against the night's darkness. As the participants went from door to door begging gifts, they would first hold the lantern against some window in the house at which they were then begging to give its occupants a special preparatory scare.

Those taking part in this practice were once more commonly known as **Hallowe'en Guisers**. They wore costumes and blackened their faces for the Vigil of All Saints. The custom virtually died out in England, though costume balls and 'trick or treating' on October 31 have gained an immense popularity in North America and its influence has been trickling back. But today's participants have little inkling of the original reasons for the costumes and the pumpkin lanterns. According to Christine Hole, these were at one time taken much more seriously. The blackened faces and the strange dress worn by the participants were an attempt to impersonate the dead. They felt that through this stratagem they would fool, and thus protect themselves from, the *real* spirits, both visible and invisible, which they believed had returned on this night.

Witchlore is especially connected with Halloween, as is reflected in a short verse which appeared in the *Denham Tracts*, published in 1895:

> *Hey-how for Hallow E'en*
> *When all the witches are to be seen,*
> *Some in black and some in green,*
> *Hey-how for Hallow E'en.*

Similarly, it was thought that children born on Halloween had the gift of second sight and could communicate with spirits. Sir Walter Scott used this belief as a device in his book *The Monastery*.

Ducking for apples on Halloween

Halloween games form an important part of this evening's entertainment; so much so that it has, in the past, acquired the names 'Crab Apple Day' and, in the north, 'Nutcrack Night'. The most famous of these games is bobbing for apples. For this, it is arranged that a large tub, full of water, and with several apples floating on its surface, confronts the children participating. The object is for them to get the apples out of the tub with their mouths. As such, hands could not be used. According to the rules, to ensure fair play, the participants' hands were often tied behind their backs. For a child, faced with a large apple, and equipped with a very small mouth, the challenge seems almost insuperable. However, there are some pointers, or secrets, involved in successful bobbing. Firstly, those apples which still have stalks attached to them are the easiest to get out. Secondly, an apple can sometimes be extracted from the tub through applying an enormous amount of suction against it. The third, but slow and sure way, is to trap the apple in a bottom corner of the tub (meaning putting one's face and head under the water) and getting a certain grip on it with the teeth, and then bringing it out. Occasionally the players were allowed to use forks, either held

179

between the teeth or dropped from above to spear the floating apples. The methods with the forks are still a challenge, but not as engaging as old fashioned bobbing.

Another popular apple game was to balance an apple and a candle on opposite ends of a board, which was then suspended from its middle by a string attached to an overhead beam. Then the candle was lit and the board spun round. The object for the players was to capture the apple with their teeth. All too often, though, they misjudged their timing and got the candle end of the stick, which meant a splattering of hot candle wax and sometimes singed hair.

There were different **Halloween superstitions**. One popular with maidens was for them to peel an apple carefully enough so that the peel came off all in one long piece. This was then thrown over the left shoulder and, when it landed on the ground, supposedly would form the initial of the girl's future husband. Another method of divination was by nuts, which are in good supply at this time. Two nuts, one representing the girl involved and the other her beloved, would be laid on, or close to, a fire. If both burnt down together, it meant their match was a good one. But if one of them exploded, or didn't burn down with the other, it was believed a sign the young lady should look elsewhere for a future partner.

Halloween brings October to a close. It has been a month of dissemination; some seeds having been sown by the farmer, and others planted willy-nilly in the wilds. Berries become especially plentiful; the hip on the rose, the haw on the hawthorn, the sloe on the blackthorn and the blackberry on the bramble. Other berries, including those of the privet, honeysuckle, elder and holly, also begin showing. There is a smell of pickling near rural homes and, in America, pumpkin pie is being baked. This was an English vegetable which the Pilgrim fathers took over to that land. The colourful local summer fare seen at the greengrocers begins to wane, and we start seeing in their displays some of those standbys which will become all too familiar through the long winter months: onions, beetroot, carrots, celery, Brussels sprouts, turnips and swedes. But, for local variety, we can look to the plentiful supply of apples, pears and a number of local nuts which are now available.

NOVEMBER

***On the first of November if the weather hold clear,
An end of wheat sowing you do for this year.***

November's name derives from its having been the ninth in the old Roman year. The Saxons, with their usual eye to the sense and significance of the season, knew it as *Wint-monath* and *Blot-monath*. *Wint-monath* refers to the high winds experienced in November, which led to their bringing their fishing boats up on shore for protection until the seas grew calmer in the next year. *Blot-monath* means 'Blood month', and its significance is easily traced to the bloody slaughtering of cattle and sheep which was customary for them during this month. The meat, once salted, was expected to see them through another winter. But the name *Blot-monath* may well have also had earlier, more sinister, derivations; in sacrificial rites which could easily have been practiced at this time of year.

After October's burst of colour, November presents us with a very sombre contrast. It has been called the gloomiest month of the year, and was once known as 'the month of blue devils and suicides'. Chill winds, a harbinger of winter, blow through the nearly bare branches on the trees, and the final leaves they had been holding on to are blown off and scattered. The last of those on the oak and beech come down towards the beginning of the month, while the greeery on the apple and peach drop nearer to its end. On young beeches, the withered leaves stay rattling on the branched through the winter, until next spring's buds finally force them off.

With all of the leaves coming down, fall is an appropriate name for this season. Ponds and ditches soon become choked with branches and leaves, and then further engorged by the rains which November's leaden skies give us. Evening arrives increasingly earlier, and frosts put an end to the last of the summer greenery.

The decline in nature reminds us of our own fleeting seasons, the theme of which was aptly expressed in Pope's Homer:

Like leaves on trees the race of man s found,

Now green in youth, now with'ring on the ground.
Another race the following spring supplies;
They fall successive, and successive rise:
So generations in their course decay,
So flourish these, when those are passed away.

Salmon go upstream to spawn, while V-shaped strings of geese fly south. Their flying pattern gives less wind resistance to those behind, but the leader, receiving its full force, soon tires and falls back to be replaced by another. Skylarks begin to be heard in November, and the wood pigeon, one of our final arrivals, comes around the middle of the month from its more northerly summer home.

November's early frosts help the dewberry, cranberry, sloe, dogwood berry and others come into their perfection. Bramble berries are a favourite for pies and homemade wine. Wild rose hips and haws, decorating the hedgerows, offer nutrition both for us and for the birds. The hard privet berries, however, are poisonous to humans, but are eaten by thrushes, who pass the seeds in their droppings.

Although this month brings some inhospitably cold weather, particularly for those of us who can remember the summer, an abundance of local produce is still available from the shops, and there are even a few new vegetables on display. Cabbages, cauliflowers, parsnips, swedes, turnips, onions, beetroot and Brussels sprouts are all on offer. Carrots and celery are near the end of their sojourn, while most greens and herbs are definitely waning. There is still consolation in an abundance of apples and pears, along with a plentiful supply of cobs, walnuts and chestnuts.

The activity of animal life has appreciably slowed down. The hedgehog, squirrel and dormouse curl up in their lairs and hibernate, having found a more sensible solution to the problem of winter than man has yet discovered. If a warmer spell comes along, they will rouse themselves and eat from their winter stores, and then fall back to sleep again when cooler weather returns. The tiny field mouse usually has the biggest larder of all. Relative to its size, its stores are veritable granaries of corn, acorns and other nuts. The ant, contrary to its industrious reputation, spends most of the winter in a fairly torpid state, having laid up no provisions whatsoever.

But all is not gloom. The autumn heather in the moorlands gives beautiful and seemingly endless views of red and gold, an especially dramatic sight in the early dusk. Branches are gathered in the woods for cheering indoor fires. There is a pleasing crunch of leaves beneath the feet and a wafting aroma of woodfires in the air. The naked trees present wonderful skeletal traceries etched against the sky.

As the fields are virtually bare now, cattle and horses are kept indoors or in the stable yard and fed from fodder. The farmer continues his ploughing and wheat-sowing. He is also busy hauling and spreading manure and fertilizers and clearing our water meadow drains and ditches.

The **Feast of All Saints**, or Omnium Sactorum Festum, is a very ancient rite celebrated on November 1. It had its roots in the Pantheon, which was erected to honour all of the Roman gods. Some said that the statues of Mars and Venus there were supposed to be representative of the legion of deities involved. Others claim the circular structure of the building was similar to that of heaven itself, and must therefore be the home of all gods. A third faction asserted that the edifice had been dedicated to Cybele, mother of gods. Whatever the reason, the name Pantheon stuck to it and meant that it commemorated all Roman deities and, perhaps, as Bede asserted, all their devils as well. The existence of such a building became an effrontery to growing Christianity and, in the seventh century, Pope Boniface IV arranged for it to be rededicated to All Saints and the Virgin Mary. Later on, Gregory IV fixed November 1 as its feast day and excluded the Virgin Mary from the celebration.

The Church felt, as there could not be a day set aside for each saint, and as so many of them remain nameless, they should be united in this way, so they could be venerated by the faithful on one single and solemn annual occasion. Its importance was such that, after the Reformation, the Feast of All Saints was retained by the Anglican Church, although many other individual saints' days were dropped.

For the Celts, November 1 was *Samhain*, the last of their quarter days and the commencement of a new year. The festival fires they lit were carried forward by the Christian Church, but ostensibly for different reasons. Church bells rang out for services through the day and, as the next day was All Souls', Souling and Soul-caking customs were enjoyed.

November 2, **All Souls' Day**, is the last in the short Hallowtide. Sacrificing to the souls of the dead had been an earlier Roman practice which they, in turn, had inherited from the Greeks. The Celtic and Teutonic peoples had similar festivals long before such services were sanctified by the Church. All Souls' Day is thought to have been formally introduced by Odilon, Abbot of Cluny in the eleventh century, but it did not achieve a general acceptance for at least another 300 years. Long before this it had been a European belief that the souls of those in Purgatory were able to return for the two days after All Hallow's Eve, and at some places it was customary to leave food out for them in the houses where they had made their earthly pilgrimages. Masses were said, and candles often lit for the dead, sometimes in the churchyards where they were buried. The wealthier had a practice of giving money to the poor as payment for the latter to do the necessary praying for their ancestors' and relatives' souls.

Just as November 1, All Saints' Day, celebrates the Church's triumphant and militant, so does the next day, All Souls', celebrate the Church's suffering. The day gained such in importance to Christians that, if the 2nd fell on a Sunday, the prayers of intercession were offered on the Saturday, rather than on the Monday following, in order that those souls involved would not be waiting the extra day.

One of the customs associated with the day was **'Souling'**, or **'Soul-caking'**, in which individuals called 'Soul-cakers' made their neighbourhood rounds, singing a souling song and requesting gifts. The alms expected were originally soulcakes, light buns which had been sweetened and spiced. Their shapes and contents varied from region to region, but they were usually flattish and round, and sometimes approached the size of a small loaf. In Yorkshire, fruitcakes were used and were known as Saumas, or Soulmas, cakes. It was believed that for each soul-cake eaten while a prayer was said, a soul would be released from Purgatory. But there were others who believed in keeping their soul-cake in their kitchens, for luck, until the next second of November.

Various souling songs were popularised. A representative one, used in Staffordshire over a hundred years ago and quoted in *British Calendar Customs: England*, included the words,

> *Remember the departed for Holy Mary's sake,*
> *And of your charity, pray gi' us a big soul-cake.*

After the Reformation, the belief in the prayer's efficacy died out, but the conviction in the value of alms-giving continued. The alms begged for changed accordingly, from the earlier soul-cakes to sweets, fruit or even money. The songs changed, too, and became more blatant in their demands, as is evidenced by one quoted in Godfrey Baseley's *A Country Compendium*:

> *You gentlemen of England, pray you now draw near*
> *To these few lines, and you soon shall hear*
> *Sweet melody of music all on this evening clear,*
>
> *Step down into your cellar and see what you can find,*
> *If your barrels are not empty, we hope you will prove kind:*
> *We hope you will prove kind with your apples and strong beer,*
> *For we'll come no more a-souling until another year.*

In some counties, notably Cheshire, the collection of alms became a costumed occasion. A Soul-Caking Play, reminiscent of the St. George's Mummers' Play, was performed on All Souls' Eve. Another Cheshire custom was the Hodening Horse, in which a man wore a horse blanket and carried a horse's skull on a pole. The jaws of the skull were hinged, allowing them to snap and some had rings of red and white paint around its eye sockets. It was taken from house to house, as a macabre pagan inheritance, in the belief it blessed the occupants with both fertility and luck. A candle lit inside it, as in the All Hallows' lanterns, added to the impression it made in the darkness.

Although, in a very few locations, children can still be seen performing their Soul-caking rounds, the Souling customs mostly fell off towards the end of the nineteenth century. They lingered on until the late 1930s at Comberbach, Cheshire, and have now been revived at the nearby village of Antrobus. The Hodening, or Hoodening, Horse was also popular in east Kent, where a wooden horses head with snapping jaws was used. Here, in some places, it has experienced a revival, and continues to offer its combined fright and blessing, especially if the visit is made on November 2.

The fifth of this month brings us one of the most remarkable and most widely celebrated of our customs, commemorating the Gunpowder Plot, in which **Guy Fawkes** and other conspirators planned to blow up King, Lords and Parliament. The plot caused an incredible wave of anti-Popish sentiment, although only a few fanatical members of that church were involved.

The gunpowder conspirators—from a print published immediately after the discovery

Roman Catholics in England had hoped there would be less persecution once James I assumed the throne. Although restrictions were relaxed during the first year of his reign, in order to keep the

Commons happy, he was obliged to reintroduce the harsher penalties which had prevailed during Elizabethan days. This received a strong reaction from a small band of Roman Catholic men. They decided to take their revenge through blowing up the legislature they held responsible for the anti-Popish rulings and, by this stratagem, seize power and return England to the Roman Catholic faith.

The men all came from good families. One of them, Robert Catesby, is credited with thinking up the idea, and another, Thomas Winter, recruited the famous Guido Fawkes. Their co-conspirator, Thomas Percy, arranged to rent the house next door to the one Parliament then met in, so that they could tunnel through to its vaults. But, although the plan had been agreed on as early as the spring of 1604, they did not begin digging until December of that year. They kept at it for some time but, all being gentlemen and unused to manual labour, it seemed an insuperable task.

Fortunately for them, while they were about this, they learned that the cellars under Parliament, which had been leased to a coal merchant for storage, were just becoming vacant. Percy arranged to rent them, and they deposited their gunpowder there on the fifth of May, 1605. The explosion was originally set for the third of October, but then changed to November 5, the date to which the next meeting of Parliament had been delayed. Guy Fawkes was given three slow-burning fuses and assigned the task of lighting them. After this, he was to escape to the Thames, wait to hear the explosion, and then make his way by boat to Flanders.

Vault beneath the old house of Lords

At this stage a dispute arose among the conspirators. Some of them wanted to warn their Catholic friends in Parliament to be absent from the meeting on the crucial day. Catesby, however, overruled them on the grounds that such warnings would seriously endanger the plot. It seems, though, that at least one member disobeyed him, for, at the end of October, the Catholic Lord Monteagle received an anonymous letter informing him that Parliament would "receyve a terrible blowe ... and yet they shall not seie who hurts them." He ignored the instructions telling him to burn the missive immediately after reading it. Instead, he passed the message on to Lord Salisbury and the King, who were able to deduce what the plot entailed. The King determined to take no action until November 5, in hopes of catching the conspirators red-handed.

The plotters, in turn, learned about the letter from a servant of Monteagle's but, as its contents had not been specific as to how their plan would operate, they went ahead, still hoping for success. On the afternoon of Monday, November 4, the Lord Chamberlain paid a visit to the cellars and discovered Fawkes there. Fawkes, using the name Johnson, and claiming to be a servant of Percy's, was still not concerned enough to abandon his plans.

But, at two o'clock on the morning of the fifth, Fawkes was caught unawares and arrested by a platoon of soldiers led by a magistrate. He was questioned by the King himself and, when he would not reveal names or details, was taken to the Tower. There he finally did talk, but only after prolonged torture on the rack. The other conspirators fled, but were pursued and captured, with the exception of Catesby and three others, who refused to surrender and were killed. Those caught were tried and executed by hanging on January 31 at St. Paul's churchyard. Fawkes went last. He was so broken from the rack that he required assistance in mounting the scaffold.

During the same month that the executions had occurred, Parliament was busy making as much political capital out of this event as possible. They passed a law making November 5 a holiday. With their approval, up until Victorian times, the *Book of Common Prayer* included a "Form of prayer with Thanksgiving for the happy deliverance of King James I. and the three estates of England from the most traitorous and bloody intended massacre by gunpowder..."

This dramatic eleventh-hour salvation of King and Parliament caught the public imagination. Even though the Gunpowder Plot itself turned out to be a non-event, it was considered the biggest victory Protestant England had experienced since the defeat of the Spanish Armada. Another reason for the public's joy at being given a new festival stemmed from the increasing influence of the Puritans, which was beginning to deprive them of so many of their old celebrations.

The Celtic Festival of Fire, which used to honour their new year, was moved forward four days and re-christened Guy Fawkes. But instead of the sacrifices which once very likely occurred at the older fire festivals, a stuffed straw Guy is now consigned to the flames.

In the few days preceding the fifth, young boys will wander the streets, carrying their Guy, or pushing him in a pram, and collecting coins from passersby. The best way to make him is to stuff some old clothes with straw, use a stick for his backbone, put a hat on his head and, to be as authentic as possible, affix three matches in one gloved hand and a lantern in the other. Placing some fireworks inside his clothes can be dangerous, but adds to the spirit of the occasion and to the dramatic effect when poor Guy finally falls into the flames. Traditional Guy Fawkes fare, afterwards, which helped ward off the chill night air, were potatoes, baked in the ashes of the fire and served up with generous dollops of butter.

Procession of a Guy

As they made their rounds begging, the boys used to sing a popular commemorative song:

Remember, Remember
The fifth of November,
Gunpowder treason and plot;
I know no reason
Why gunpowder treason
Should ever be forgot.

A stick and a stake
For King James's sake,
Then hollow boys, hollow boys,
God save the King.

A stick and a stump
For Guy Fawkes' rump;
The hollow boys, hollow boys,
God save the King.
Huzza—a—a!

Chambers, writing in the early 1860s, describes the near maniacal fervour of earlier Guy Fawkes celebrations:

"In former times in London, the burning of the effigy of Guy Fawkes on the fifth of November was a most important and portentous ceremony. The bonfire in Lincoln's Inn Fields was conducted on an especially magnificent scale. Two hundred cart-loads of fuel would sometimes be consumed in feeding this single fire, while upwards of thirty 'Guys' would be suspended on gibbets and committed to the flames. Another tremendous pile was heaped up by the butchers in Clare market, who on the same evening paraded through the streets in great force, serenading the citizens with the famed 'marrow-bone-and-cleaver' music. The uproar throughout the town from the shouts of the mob, the ringing of the bells in churches, and the general confusion which prevailed, can but faintly be imagined by an individual of the present day."

Another custom was that of **'Swinging the Guy'**. Swinging in this case meant stealing, and involved youths, who did not have the means or inclination to make their own Guys, setting upon and stealing a Guy from a weaker group. Battles also arose when two groups carrying rival Guys met on the streets.

In the course of the now more than four hundred years that Guys have been put to the torch, the stuffed dummy used has often represented someone else, whom the celebrants considered to be a more real current threat to England. As the original conspirators were Roman Catholics, a 'Guy' wearing a mitre was common, and the day became known in some localities as 'Pope Day'. Until relatively recently in Lewes, Sussex, where Protestant martyrs had been put to death under Mary I, there were two bonfires, one each for the effigies of the Guy and the Pope. The figure of Pope Paul IV has been used, too, as he was erroneously thought to have encouraged the Gunpowder Plot. After what was considered Papal aggression in 1850, Cardinal Wiseman, first Archbishop of Westminster, was burnt.

Non-religiousfigures have also been popular: Napoleon during his wars; Nan Sahib and the Sultan of Turkey after their respective atrocities in Cawnpore and Armenia; Kruger during the Boer War; and the Kaiser and Hitler during the first and second world wars. Probably the best dummy ever consigned to the flames on November the fifth occurred when ex-servicemen burned an effigy labelled simply 'War' during the 1920s.

Except in a very few locations, the wild exuberance of Bonfire Night has now been contained and controlled by the authorities. Fireworks are, more often than not, burnt safely at a distance by the local police or by the fire brigade. But many of the earlier practices were often so boisterous as to be violent and dangerous. In some places flaming tar-barrels were kicked through the streets. Jacqueline Simpson notes that at Rye, Sussex, Guy Fawkes Day at one time was used as an excuse to tar and feather others the townsfolk had been nursing grudges against.

Spirited celebrations are yet observed at Lewes, Sussex, and at Bridgwater, Somerset. But in both of these towns Bonfire Committee now make and control most of the arrangements. The practice of **'Rolling of the Tar Barrels'** at Ottery St. Mary, Devon, is one of the most novel and dangerous still extant. Here, a number of burning tar-barrels are carried through the street by young men in turns. Their arms are swathes in protective material, but even then they must drop their loads, scattering burning tar around them. A local regional newspaper, the, reported not long ago,

> The 'rolling' is an incredible spectacle as men swathe themselves in sacking and lift blazing barrels of tar on to their shoulders to run through the streets.
> It is as dangerous as it is breath-taking, and many is the

participant and spectator who have been singed by the flames.
- *Express & Echo*, 12 July 1983

The custom seems almost a rite of manhood, and recalls the pagan practice of people leaping through the *Samhain* bonfires to purify themselves for the new year.

Parliament had also ordered that church bells be rung on the fifth as part of the holiday observances. The day accordingly became known as **'Ringing Night'** in many villages. It continues so at Spelsbury, Oxfordshire, where a bequest of land was left by a Protestant Royalist to finance the bell ringing on this night and on Oak Apple Day (May 29).

Another custom which emanated from the Gunpowder Plot, but which does not occur on November 5, is **searching the Houses of Parliament**, a dignified search through the cellars of the present building by the Yeomen of the Guard on the eve of the morning before they are opened each year.

In the Midlands and North, and particularly in Yorkshire, Halloween pranks, played by the high-spirited young, were moved forward to Guy Fawkes Eve, which acquired the name **'Mischief Night'**.

From our modern vantage point, Guy Fawkes celebrations almost appear an anachronism. For many it represents a sentiment of violence nurtured between Protestant and Roman Christians, which we have surely outgrown by now. It should be kept in mind, as Laurence Whistler points out, that although the custom remembers a serious attempt at treason by one Roman Catholic, Guy Fawkes, the Gunpowder Plot was foiled by the loyalty of another, Lord Monteagle.

Yet there are very good arguments for the continuation of this festival. Now that many of the Hollowtide customs have fallen into disuse, there is very little in the way of landmarks in the rural calendar between Michaelmas and Christmas, and even the former of these is now little observed, except for the expiration and renewal of tenancies.

Guy Fawkes Day has a sentiment of national unity about it, which also lends itself to approval in these otherwise divisive times. Finally, it should be remembered that, in real life, Guy Fawkes was hanged, not burnt, and that the bonfires and fireworks enjoyed today probably owe much more, although perhaps mostly now on an unconscious level, to the thousands of years of ancient Festivals of Fire, than they do to a failed Gunpowder Plot.

After the great national outburst on the fifth, there are little more than a handful of saints' days to relieve the rest of November's leaden skies, chill winds and increasingly shorter days. The best known of these is **Martinmas**'s on the eleventh. **St. Martin of Tours** was born in Sabaria, now part of Yugoslavia, about 315. His father was a Roman military tribune and, although the boy Martin had a very gentle disposition, he was enrolled at an early age in the imperial horse guards, and stayed in the army until he was forty. Although he wanted to preach in France, St. Hilary of Poitiers advised him first to convert his own family. In this he was successful only with his mother. After living in solitude for several years at Milan, he returned to Poitiers and founded a monastery. He became Bishop of Tours about 374 and had a wide-ranging influence on the populace, converting virtually everyone within his travelling sphere from paganism, as well as destroying the old temples. Martin died about 397.

The most famous legend connected with this saint grew from an experience he had while still in the Roman army. It tells of him having given half of his cloak to a naked beggar at the city of Amiens. Later on, in a vision that night, Martin saw Christ, dressed in the identical half of his cloak which had been given to the mendicant. He heard Christ say to the surrounding angels, "Martin, although he is only a catechumen [one who is still preparing for baptism in the Church], gave me this cloak."

St. Martin dividing his cloak with a beggar

There is a story claiming that St. Martin's famous cloak was kept at Tours. A cloak then was known there as a *chape*, or *capella* in Latin. The French oratory which guarded this relic is said to have acquired the name *chappelle*, and those responsible for its safe-keeping similarly became known as *chapelains*. There is a claim that the English words 'chapel' and 'chaplain' came from this same root. Another word deriving from the saint, at one time common in northern England and Scotland, was 'mart', which meant a fatted ox. The association arose from beeves being slaughtered on or near Martinmas to provide food for the winter.

Because of his mission in France, St. Martin has gained an immense popularity. It is estimated that about four thousand churches are dedicated to him there, and that close to five hundred French villages have been named after him. Partly as a result of the Norman Conquest, Martin has also become a prominent saint in England, and many of our churches have been dedicated to him. Martinmas is still considered a quarter-day in Scotland and, like Michaelmas, it was a common date set for rent payments and for the termination of tenancies.

One similar payment custom continues to be held at Knightlow Cross near Dunchurch, in Warwickshire, just before dawn on November eleventh. The money paid is called **Wroth Silver** and payment is made by representatives of the different parishes of the Knightlow Hundred to the Lord of the Hundred, Duke Buccleuch. At Knightmow Cross, the Charter of Assembly is read, and the money, a very little amount in today's terms, is placed on the small bit of what is left of the cross. Afterwards, those making payment are provided with a hearty breakfast at the Duke's expense. The custom is so ancient that the exact reason for the payment has been forgotten. One theory has it that it was in return for the right to take cattle across the Dunsmore Heath, while another suggests the payments were made to exempt members of the parishes concerned from military services. One of the heavy penalties exacted for non-payment also attests to the antiquity of this custom. Parishes defaulting must either pay a fine, which is several times the value of the Wroth Silver, or give the Duke a white bull with red ears. Although a bull of this type is thought to have been common in our wild cattle centuries ago, it is a very rare commodity in these days.

In some regions Martinmas, or the day after it, acquired the name **Pack Rag Day**. At these locations, male and female servants would leave their employers and look for work elsewhere. Presumably, the employer they were leaving had been so miserly that all they had to pack were rags. It would be interesting to see the results of a revival of this particular custom. One wonders how many tens of thousands (if not more!) of dissatisfied urban employees would quit their jobs, if all concerned understood and agreed that it could be done honourably on this one day each year ...and that there would be a new job with a better new employer awaiting!

November twenty-third is **St. Clement's Day**. He was the third Bishop of Rome after Peter and received mention in Paul's Philippians. Legend has it that he was martyred about 100 AD by being weighed down with an anchor and thrown into the Black Sea. An unreliable saying, *"St. Clement gives the winter"*, attached itself to this day, implying that the weather on the twenty-third would be a foretaste of that of winter.

Clement became the patron saint of blacksmiths, who used to celebrate his day with a noisy evening feast. Sometimes they paraded through their towns during the day, carrying an 'Old Clem' effigy and asking for donations which would be put toward the celebratory dinner. Children later imitated these tradesmen and used the occasion to go 'Clementing', asking for apples, pears or a penny, and singing a Clemeny song. Although Clementing processions pretty much died out in the nineteenth century, St. Clement's day is still celebrated in some rural villages.

St. Catherine, whose day falls two days later, was often linked with

Clement in similar Cattern and Clement processions and rhymes. In fact, Catherine was the more popular of the two, probably because of the greater number of trades she had patronage over. She is reputed to have been sentenced to be crushed between four spiked wheels in fourth century Alexandria, Egypt, but the wheels splintered to bits as soon as she was tied to them. It is said the pagan emperor Maxentius then executed her himself by cutting her head off with a sword. As a result of the tools used in her martyrdom, Catherine is associated with both the sword and the wheel. The circular window seen in churches is known as a Catherine-wheel window, and a famous firework has also been named after her.

There are about 80 churches dedicated to St. Catherine in England. She became patron saint of all who worked with wheels, including spinners, turners, millers, wheelwrights and grinders. She was also, in some countries, the patron saint of lace-makers, who enjoyed the twenty-fifth as a day of rest. Spinners also often celebrated Catherine's Day with processions, merrymaking and the eating of a Cattern cake. It is probably due to the original meaning of the word spinster having been associated with the latter trade that single girls at one time were wont to make special prayers for a husband to this virgin saint.

Another saint who became a more widely accepted protector of lace-makers is Andrew, patron saint of Scotland. **St. Andrew**, whose feast day is November thirtieth, is considered to have been the first of Christ's disciples, after having previously been one to John the Baptist. He was joined almost immediately by his brother Simon Peter. Andrew is thought to have been martyred on an upside-down or diagonally-shaped cross at Patras, Greece, about AD 64, and the saltire cross has accordingly become his emblem. November 30 was a holiday for lace-makers in a number of adjoining counties just northwest of London, including Buckinghamshire, Bedfordshire, Northamptonshire and Hertfordshire. It acquired the name Tandry, or Tandering, Day. Specially prepared cakes and buns eaten then were known as 'St. Andrew's Buns' or 'Tandry Wigs', and the saint was toasted with hot elderberry wine. Part of the festivities involved men dressing up in women's clothes and women in men's. Schoolchildren celebrated the occasion by barring their schoolmaster out of the school. These festivities never entered the twentieth century, but a saw which was associated with the day still holds true,

St. Andrew the King
Three weeks and three days before Christmas comes in.

Although he is much more celebrated in Scotland, St. Andrew's importance in England derives mostly from the fact that the Sunday nearest his feast day is **Advent**, which has been the beginning of the Christian ecclesiastical year for the last fourteen centuries. Advent means approach or arrival, and the Sunday is designated to be the first of those four which immediately precede the joys of Christmas. Advent, being always the closest Sunday to November 30, whether before or after, can occur from November 27 to December 3.

With Advent's promise of Christmas, there is an end in the gloomy frame of mind November so often has left us with, even though this Sunday's celebrations may fall in the latter days of that month. The period of 'blue devils and suicides' is over, and a time of preparation has begun. In northern England, in days now past, it was customary for the poor to carry, in a box known as a Vessel Cup, often with a glass lid covered with a white cloth, the **advent images** of the baby Christ and the Virgin Mary. After the payment of some alms, the figures were uncovered and were believed to carry a spiritual blessing to those who saw them.

Today, with the beginning which is Advent, we, too, start preparations for Christmas. Indeed, it would be hard not to, inundated as we are with reminders from all the media. In an external sense, we think about which presents we will get for whom and of buying and preparing special foods and drink to mark the occasion. Decorations are unpacked and put up, and the first doors and windows of Advent calendars are opened. Most especially, we look forward to experiencing togetherness in families which are often otherwise separated by great geographical distances during the rest of the year.

But Advent is a time of internal, or spiritual, preparation, too. It is a reminder of the forthcoming birthday of Christian spirituality itself on earth, the occurrence of which was considered of such importance by the ancient church fathers as to have been set to coincide with the life-giving sun's own regeneration.

DECEMBER

December frost and January flood
Never boded husbandman good.

As in the preceding three months, the Romans called this one after its position, tenth in this case, in their year. Our Anglo-Saxon forefathers knew it by the more individual peculiarities which distinguished December from the rest of the natural cycle. They called it *Winter-monath* for the season it introduces. After the early Church fathers had converted them, they rechristened it *Heligh-monath*, or Holy Month, as it contained the important feast of Christmas. Some even knew it as *Christmonat*, although that appellation was more characteristic of those Teutonic peoples who had remained in Germany.

December is one of our most unpleasant months weather-wise. The increasingly cooler temperatures bring fog at its beginning and frost and snow towards its end. This air of gloom is enhanced by shorter and shorter days until, with the shortest; there is less than eight hours of daylight left. One of the cheerier experiences in this month is to come in from the cold and see a warm fire blazing in the hearth and the steam rising from a hot dinner. The scene and the comforts available are aptly described in a verse from *Poor Robin's Almanack*,

> *Now trees their leafy hats do bare,*
> *To reverence Winter's silver hair;*
> *A handsome hostess, merry host,*
> *A pot of ale now and a toast,*
> *Tobacco and good coal fire,*
> *Are things this season doth require.*

Icicles hang by the window, and the vicar's Sunday sermon is all too frequently interrupted by coughing fits brought on by the cold weather. Children, it seems, are the only ones who greet the first snowfall with enthusiasm. They are impatient for the joys of building snowmen, sliding on ponds, skating and fighting snowball battles.

The little left of our contingent of birds appear both cold and starved. The robin is one of the few which might still be heard singing. The owl, however, has a different attitude to winter, and can usually be found, with its feathers fluffed out, in the hollow of a tree. The wren and titmouse shelter from the winds by hiding in ivy-covered walls, while the blackbird often seeks refuge from the cold in barns and sheds. Food for the birds becomes more and more of a problem. Some used to try to make a meal from the top of the thatched hayricks. Others, like the wood-pigeon, manage somehow on what is left of the winter greens. Larks, if permitted, will gorge themselves in the newly sown cornfields. Fortunately for them, birds need much less food now, as they sleep about twice as long in the winter as they did in the summer.

December is a relatively quiet month on the farm. With the last of the wheat having been sown, much of the month is spent in ploughing and manure-spreading. Lambing pens are also knocked together, mostly in the southern counties. In the latter part of the month, sheep which have not been taken into the fold have at least their natural blanket of wool to cover them as they burrow down into the snow for the little sustenance still left in the fields. December can be a profitable time for the astute husbandman, who sends his poultry and fat stock to the Christmas markets.

In anticipation of the coming festive celebrations, the early days of December are a time when housewives are busy preparing their puddings and pies. The greengrocers give us a selection of fruits and vegetables which is quite extraordinary for this time of year. Much of it now, though, is imported and has little to do with our own crops.

Where there is snow, except for the traces left in footprints in it wildlife seems to have vanished. The hedgehog and badger have retired to their lairs to sleep until spring. Having laid up no stores, they must wait for nature herself to wake and furnish their next meal. Squirrels and mice also spend most of the winter sleeping, though they rouse themselves occasionally to nibble from provisions set by in autumn. The fox is one of winter's more active creatures, and used to be notorious for daring midnight raids on the henhouse.

With the onset of much colder temperatures, plants which have not died have virtually ceased growing. Mosses and lichens are some of the few which still seem to flourish in December's chill. They can be admired all the more now that the distracting greenery of the trees is no longer in evidence. Various evergreens, especially the holly, acquire new life in contrast to their bare neighbours, while, in the kitchen garden, parsley, savoy and kale are among the few hardy survivors. The mistletoe, an emblem of Druidic fertility, can be found on hawthorn and apple trees, but rarely on their sacred oak. In the entire plant kingdom, perhaps the most symbolic and optimistic sign of hope comes from the Glastonbury Thorn, which will flower late in this month or early in January. Its symbolism is enhanced by the simultaneous display of both flower and fruit, for berries from its first blossoming in May will often be seen cheek-by-jowl with the new buds.

St. Nicholas, whose feast day is December 6, is probably the most renown and popular saint throughout the Christian world. He is the patron saint of children, pawnbrokers, sailors, virgins, thieves and of what remains of Christian Russia. Nearly 400 English churches are dedicated to him.

Nicholas was the fourth century Bishop of Myra in Asia Minor. Little is known for sure of his history, except that he was indubitably a real person. He is thought to have attended the Council at Nicaea in 325, and to have died in 342. In the spirit of the Crusades, a group of pious businessmen removed St. Nicholas's relics from Myra towards the end of the eleventh century and re-deposited them in the Church of St. Stephen in Bari, Italy. His fame grew through the numerous legends which are associated with him, and it is from one of these that one of our most cherished annual customs derives.

It seems that in his day at Myra there were three girls of a good, but impoverished family. Having no dowry to tempt potential suitors, their father was finally faced with two options. His daughters would have to earn their living as prostitutes or they would all starve to death. News of their predicament reached Nicholas, and he determined to save the girls from their impending degradation. He approached their house late at night and threw three bags of gold in through an open window. The gift gave the distressed father sufficient dowry for all three of his daughters to marry.

Nicholas's patronage over virgins stems from this legend. The three bags of gold are also thought to have been the origin of the three gold balls forming the emblem of the pawnbrokers' sign, as well as of the Florence Medici's family crest. But a far more important tradition grew out of this particular story. It became a practice for younger children in families, and even for boarders at convents, to awake on December 6 and find their shoes or stockings filled with sweets and small gifts. The surprises, having arrived secretly, almost magically, in the night, led to their being attributed to the beneficence of St. Nicholas.

The custom grew especially strong in Holland and in Dutch colonies. They often celebrate with a St. Nicholas procession towards the end of November, in which the saint is dressed in his bishop's robes and mitre, and attended to by his Negro servant, Black Peter. Dutch immigrants to America perpetuated the custom there. It was thought to be so charming that it gained widespread favour with all but the most puritanical Americans in New York State. However, non-Dutch Americans felt it a more appropriate practice to observe in conjunction with their Christmas, and duly moved it forward nineteen days. The Dutch '*St. Nicholaas*' gradually transformed itself, by word of children's mouths, to the now much loved Santa Claus, who has inherited all of the more ancient traditions which were once associated with the Norse god Woden, Old Father Christmas and the German Kris Kringle. As a result of their popularity in America, Santa Claus practices gradually caught on in England towards the middle of the nineteenth century. Even today, partly because of the tremendous media build-up it receives, it remains one of the most important celebrations which have come to us from, or through, a former colony.

Another legend, which was once prominent in English calendar customs, related to the reasons for St. Nicholas being patron saint of children. In this one, two boys, sons of a wealthy Asian, were on their way to study in Athens. However, their father had admonished them to stop in Myra on the way, in order to receive Bishop Nicholas's blessing. As they arrived there late in the evening, they stopped for the night at a local inn, intending to see the saint on the following day. The innkeeper, sensing a profit, murdered them both, cut up their bodies and tried to disguise his crime by putting the pieces into a pickling vat along with some pork. According to which version of the legend one refers to, Nicholas either heard the boys cry out as he was passing, or had a vision of what had happened. He confronted the landlord, and the latter owned up to his crime. According to Chambers, at this point Nicholas is supposed to have approached the tub containing the boys' remains and to have

> "made the sign of the cross and offered up a supplication for their resurrection to life. Scarcely was the saint's prayer finished when the detached and mangled limbs were miraculously reunited, and the two youths regaining animation, rose up alive in the tub, and threw themselves at the feet of their benefactor. We are further informed that the archbishop refused their homage, desiring the young men to return their thanks to the proper quarter from which that blessing had descended; and then, after giving them his benediction, he dismissed them with great joy to continue their journey to Athens."

St. Nicholas – From a Bodleian Library MS

This legend has resulted in Nicholas often being portrayed in his bishop's robes next to a tub full of naked children. The saint's identification with children led to the election of a **Boy Bishop** on December 6 in many English parishes. The young prelate would perform a bishop's real duties, with the exception of celebrating mass, until December 28, Holy Innocents' Day. On his last day in office, he would preach a sermon and lead a procession through the town, before surrendering his robes and mitre. During his term he was treated with the reverence due a real bishop and, if he died in office,

he was given a funeral and interment appropriate to his high post. A monument in the north side of Salisbury Cathedral's nave purports to honour one such Boy Bishop, and a similar one can be seen at the parish church of Filey, Yorkshire. Except for a short revival during the reign of Mary I, the Boy Bishop tradition died out in England after the Protestant Reformation.

Before the switch to the Gregorian calendar, December 13, **St. Lucy's Day**, was considered the date of the winter solstice. A proverb, the obverse of the one used on St. Barnabas's Day (June 11), was popularised,

> *Lucy light, Lucy light,*
> *The shortest day and the longest night.*

Lucy was a native of Syracuse in Sicily. She is supposed to have had a very persistent suitor, who was enraged at her devotion to chastity and choice of the religious life. He denounced her to the governor of Syracuse, who had Lucy martyred for her Christian beliefs in 304.

December 13 also marks the **last of the year's four Ember-Days**. These had been observed first under Pope Calixtus in the third century, when four periods of fasting as a means of bringing a blessing on the harvest were set aside. They were also used by the clergy as a spiritual aid preparatory to ordination, in line with the apostolic fast described in *Acts*, chapter 13. In Latin, the Ember-Days became known as *Jejunia quator temporum*, or 'the fasts of the four seasons.' According to our own *Book of Common Prayer*, the fasting (less quantity of food) with abstinence (less quality of food, usually meaning no meat) is supposed to be observed on December 13 and in connection with the three other Ember-Days; being the Wednesday, Friday and Saturday after the first Sunday in Lent, the Feast of Pentecost and September 14.

After the change from the Julian calendar, the solstice fell on December 21, the feast day of **St. Thomas**, and the couplet which had been used on St. Lucy's Day was duly revised,

Thomas, who was known in Greek as Didymus, was the famous doubting apostle. So convinced was he of the apparent success of the crucifixion that he did not bother to see Jesus with the other disciples on the evening of the original Easter. Even when he was told of the joyful news of the Resurrection, he said, "Except I shall see in his hands the print of the nails, and put my finger into the print of the nails, and thrust my hand into his side, I will not believe." When he was offered a chance to put Jesus to his test, his simple confession "My Lord and my God" is apt for both its sincerity and its brevity. This apostle, whose story, more than any other's, underlines the indisputable evidence of the Resurrection, is an appropriate one to crown the winter solstice, when nature itself is on the brink of rebirth. Thomas, too, with his fears and confusion, is one of the more suitable saints worth remembering in our present doubting age. He was an important enough saint to have a festival instituted in his honour in the twelfth century. This may, in part, have been meant to replace the earlier pagan feast of Thor, which was celebrated in conjunction with the winter solstice. The Saxons also held a vigil at their solstice, but for them it was known as Night of Mothers, or Mother-Night.

It was tradition for poorer people to beg alms from door to door on December 21. The custom was variously known as **'Thomassing'**, **'Going a-gooding'**, **'Doleing'**, and **'Mumping'**. In Warwickshire it was called **'Going a corning'** as that was the gift most often proffered. With winter having now begun in earnest, the alms received from Thomassing must have made a considerable difference in the Christmas provisions enjoyed by the poor. Tradition in some regions deemed that they present each of their benefactors with a sprig of mistletoe or holly. At the great houses spiced ale was prepared for a celebration on St. Thomas's Night, and it is reputed that, of those who came to enjoy it, many had so much that they were unable to make their way back home again. However, with the improvement in conditions and the establishment of other charities, there was less extreme poverty, and the Thomassing forages gradually died out towards the very end of the nineteenth century.

Although by our present calendar, we are now nearing the very end of our year, there has been an emotional and, hopefully, spiritual build-up in anticipation of the most widely celebrated feast day in the whole Christian year. Unlike Easter, the Nativity has not been observed since the time of Christ, and the history of its gradual growth through the centuries is a curious one.

The actual date of Christ's birth is not known, but it is thought unlikely to have been in the winter when, even in Palestine, cattle and sheep were kept indoors. The year itself is in doubt. The present error in that seems due to miscalculations on the part of a sixth century monk, Dionysius Exiguus, who omitted to place the year 0 between 1 BC and 1 AD, and overlooked the fact that Herod, who was in power when Jesus was born, had died in 4 BC.

J.A.R. Pimlott observes that birthdays were not celebrated in New Testament times.   Origen, as late as the third century, considered birthday remembrances to be a heathen practice and notes that, in the Bible, Herod and the Pharaoh are the only ones mentioned who celebrated their natal dates. Pimlott goes on to postulate the sensible theory that the early Christians must have been far more interested in anticipating the promised second coming than in looking back to the first.

The earliest documents which mention December 25 being known as **Christmas** Day date from the decades just after the Council of Nicaea in 325. Even then it did not become an official holiday for another two centuries. Its positioning owes much more to earlier pagan celebrations which occurred at this time of year than to the authentic original birth date of Jesus. Midwinter festivals are known to have been observed in Babylon, Egypt and Rome long before the beginning of the Christian era, and undoubtedly antedate recorded history. Germanic peoples, too, had enjoyed their festival of *Yule* with the winter solstice.

Common practices running through most of these customs were those of lighting great fires and of putting up evergreen decorations. It is thought that the fires, as with those lit on Midsummer's Eve, were meant to help strengthen and encourage the dying sun, while the evergreens gave a hopeful glimpse towards a new spring.

The very early church frowned on such idolatry. Laurence Whistler quotes the theologian Tertullian who, writing about AD 200, said, 'Let those who have no light in themselves light candles! ...Let those over whom Hell fire is hanging fix to their doors laurels doomed presently to burn! You are the light of the world, you are the tree ever green. If you have renounced temples make not your own house a temple."

The decision to fix the Nativity to the 25th of this month owed most to the various Roman customs which clustered about this date. The major one was their festival of Saturnalia, a riotous week extending from December 17 to 24. Aside from the preparation of food, work was forbidden, and master and slave became equals to enjoy a period of feasting, drinking, dancing and games.

The Romans celebrated the day following Saturnalia, the 25th, as *Dies Natalis Invicta*, 'Birthday of the Unconquered Sun'. It was a Mithraic feast, marking the birthday of the Roman soldier's patron god. By about the third century, when Mithraism had become a particularly strong rival to growing Christianity, the Church fathers were eager to set the Nativity on a date which would strengthen Christ's appeal to pagan worshippers by associating His arrival with that of the new sun.

In spite of the symbolic importance of this date, there was still some internal dissension concerning it. In the same century that Roman Christians began celebrating December 25 as Christmas Day, the Eastern Church is known to have observed the Nativity and Epiphany on January fifth and sixth. The stress they laid on the Epiphany may have partly derived from an earlier heretic, Basilides, who, in the second century, taught that Christ's divinity did not date from his birth, but from his baptism. Although the Council at Tours in 567 attempted to settle the controversy by recognising the Twelve Days between December 25 and January 6 as a period of sacred festival, the Orthodox Eastern Church still today hold to a Christmas placed alongside the later Epiphany.

The observance of a Christian Nativity in Anglo-Saxon England would have had its first significant impact through the mission of St. Augustine. He had had his instructions from Pope Gregory to

Christianise their heathen festivals rather than essay the impossible job of stopping them altogether. In this way, the earliest English Christmases became grafted onto the earlier Teutonic *Yule* practices, which are thought to have included evergreen decorations, mumming pageants, feasting, drinking, games, and their traditional Yule log.

Preparations for the Feast of Nativity are lengthy, their commencement having been set by the Church at Advent, the fourth Sunday before Christmas. We should remember, though, that the preparation intended was meant to be a spiritual one. It is an easy thing to forget today, when the temporal side of the feast so often seems to take precedence.

Decorations have always been an important part of the secular preparations. Flowers and green boughs had been perennial favourites, even before the advent of Christianity. The English traditionally used holly, ivy, bay, laurel, rosemary and boughs from the holm oak and other evergreens. However, one of the earlier favourites, the pagan mistletoe, was banned from all churches, except for York Cathedral, where it is presumed that a concentration of Druidic worship was much more deeply established than elsewhere. Mistletoe has, however, continued to be displayed in homes during this season and, from its ancient association with fertility, we have inherited our custom of stealing a kiss beneath it.

The **Christmas tree**, which we now almost universally associate with this season, is a relatively new immigrant to England. It had originated in Germany. Although the first written reference to one seems to date from the very early seventeenth century, the practice is undoubtedly much older and connected with the other greenery used at this time. There are sixteenth century references which indicate it had been derived from the Tree of Life used in medieval plays about the Garden of Eden. Later, with Luther's enthusiastic support, the Christmas tree gained its first popularity in other Protestant countries. It became a part of Christmas celebrations in America, predominantly in Pennsylvania and other areas where there were large German settlements, almost one hundred years before it caught on in England.

While there are isolated instances of Christmas trees in the English homes of German visitors or immigrants since as early as 1821, the custom did not catch the public imagination until 1841, when Prince Albert introduced the first lighted and decorated Royal tree at Windsor Castle. Dickens referred to it as a "pretty German toy" in an article he wrote in 1854. Today, most village greens or town centres sport a large lighted tree, adding a festive air and focal point for carollers. The most famous and, by now, traditional tree is the one set up annually, now on the first Thursday in December, in Trafalgar Square, which has been a gift from the citizens of Oslo to the citizens of London since 1947.

The Christmas tree's popularity soon eclipsed and replaced the older and traditionally native Kissing Bough, which used to be hung from the centre of most living-room ceilings. These were made with half or whole spheres of iron hoops which had greenery twisted around them. Apples were hung from the hoops, candles set on them and, from the centre, a branch or sprig of mistletoe descended. In some regions, the bough became known as 'the mistletoe', even when that plant did not make up part of the arrangement. The candles were lit on Christmas Eve and on each night of its Twelve Days. The light they shed on the apples may have been intended to represent that of the reborn sun's on its family of planets. Kissing under it between all classes was customarily permitted, and carollers would encircle it to sing their songs.

Sadly, this particularly native decoration is only rarely seen today. A revival of the Kissing Bough would make, as Laurence Whistler points out, a beautiful and symbolic adjunct to our newer arrival, the Teutonic Christmas tree.

The **Christmas card** is another preliminary to the season that we are all too aware of today. It was a Victorian invention, though it had been customary in upper and middle classes before then to convey the season's greetings to absent family and friends on special notepaper which was embossed or headed with an appropriate design or poem.

Published at Summersby's Home Treasury Office
12 Old Bond Street, London.

While there are different claims to the first Christmas card, it is generally accepted that one designed for Henry Cole by John Calcott Horsley in 1843 wins that honour. It showed a family seated around a table, toasting the absent friend the card was being sent to. On each side panel to this central picture were scenes of acts of charity befitting the spirit of the feast day the card commemorates.

Cole's cards had to be hand-coloured and cost an expensive shilling apiece. Only about one thousand copies were printed, and the few which have survived command extremely high prices from collectors these days. It seems, though, that the fad did not begin to catch on until twenty years later, when commercial printers began to offer greeting cards which one could colour or decorate oneself.

The reason for the steady growth in the cards since then is easily understood by today's recipients. If received early enough, it clamours for a response ...or a feeling of guilt. The early contagion in the exchange of Christmas cards is noted in records of the Post Office from the 1870s, when they began to have to hire extra help during the Christmas season. Their comments infer that the mania for sending Christmas greetings was then approaching that which they had already experienced for St. Valentine's Day.

In the 1880s, leading artists were commissioned to design the most tasteful and suitable of Christmas cards, but it is notable that, during that decade, two of the leading quality English printers decided not to continue with the product, when they realised the public was mostly interested in inferior mass-produced cards. Indeed, many of these early commercial Christmas cards had been St. Valentine's Day ones with the verse changed to fit the new occasion.

A number of the first proper Christmas cards, and this is true of some still seen today, feature the robin, for that bird is one of the very few which might be heard singing during this season. But, more importantly, its puffed and bright little red breast formed an appropriately symbolic emblem for a major solar festival.

A rather sad commentary on the importance secular aspects have assumed in the observance of the Nativity is noted by Pimlott. He refers to an authority who has remarked that the very small proportion of these early Christmas cards which had religious themes was still equalled by a similar proportion as recently as the 1950s. Pimlott points out, however, that the design of Christmas cards is probably more in the psychologist's province than in that of the historian. In spite of this, according to his very thorough *The Englishman's Christmas*, religious and spiritual interest in Christmas *did* gain a tremendous impetus from the rather crass, but immensely popular, secular customs. Crassness aside, one can still find the occasional attractive and appropriate card which truly expresses the real sentiment of the occasion it celebrates. All too often, though, it can appear as a neglected item on a store's shelf, but sometimes - more delightfully - arrives to surprise one in the post, perhaps hand-made by a sender who could find nothing suitable for sale.

The rounds of carollers in the streets, as well as the songs heard in church and through the media, also help to put us into a suitable mood for the season. The earliest carols heard in England came from the continent, and are thought to have had their origins in

French dance songs. Our first recorded medieval carol dates from the thirteenth century and is written in the French which was then peculiar to Normandy. Wynken de Worde published an English collection of **Christmas carols** as early as 1521. The differences between these first ones and those we sing today can be seen from the first verse of one called "I saw a Fair Mayden", dating from 1396,

> *I saw a fair Mayden syttin' and sing.*
> *She lullyd a lytel child, a swete lording,*
> *Lullay myn lyking, my dere sone, myne sweeting,*
> *Lullay my dere herte, myne own dere darling.*

Carols flourished from about the time of Chaucer. Their themes, which stressed charity, goodwill and merriness, had an immense appeal to the vast illiterate medieval populace. The Church sanctioned them as a method of bringing the message of the Nativity to even the humblest of parishioners.

However, a good number of the songs were not restricted to religious teaching, but instead celebrated common life and the enjoyment of the season. This frivolity, along with the sanction carols received from the Church of Rome, made them an effrontery to the Puritans. The Reverend Robert Herrick must have written what were nearly the last of our early serious carols just before Cromwell's men relieved him of his parish in 1647. An improvement in style over the fourteenth century carols can be seen in the first verse of one of these later ones, written in 1640 by Richard Crashaw,

> *The gloomy night embraced the place*
> *Wherein the noble infant lay;*
> *The Babe look'd up and shoed his face,*
> *In spite of darkness it was day,*
> *It was Thy day, sweet, and did rise*
> *Not from east, but from Thine eyes.*

For the next two centuries carols were banned from churches and frowned upon in the better houses. Fortunately, the lower classes, unimpressed by Puritan austerity, kept the carolling custom up round their own hearths. Even as late as 1834, Mary Howitt, in her *Pictorial Calendar of the Seasons*, comments in a section called an

"Antiquarian Notice" for Christmas,

> "In the present day the place of the carols is supplied by tunes played just before midnight …, whilst the carols themselves are annually published in the humblest form and with the coarsest wood-cuts for the amusement of the people. On the Christmas Day these carols used to take the place of psalms in the churches, and more particularly at the afternoon service, the whole congregation joining in them."

The tunes she refers to were played by publicly appointed musicians or professional touring companies known as **Waits**. The performers, usually wind instrumentalists, had evolved from the minstrels who played at the King's Court. Waits appointed by cities and towns date from as early as 1400. They played their music in the streets during the two to three week period before Christmas, and expected donations for their efforts. The custom died out in the last half of the nineteenth century, mostly because the donations shrank to too small an amount to make it worth the trouble. Another reason for the decline stemmed from the fact that too many amateur musicians, some of whom had never seen a musical instrument before, toured the streets in an effort to cash in on the tradition's charitable side.

Christmas Morning Carol by Children in Yorkshire

Carols were finally re-established in the Victorian era, following the new interest in Christmas which had been revived with the institution of the Christmas tree and the seasonal greeting card. The Church of England was the first to allow carols to be sung within its walls. Soon, with the surge in evangelism, the custom also spread rapidly through the Nonconformist sects.

But, even so, many still looked down on the humble carol. Chambers, in 1864, says,

> "It will be recollected that Goldsmith's Vicar of Wakefield, describing the unsophisticated character of his parishioners, says 'they kept up the Christmas carol.' Such a composition as the following might have been sung by these simple swains. It is one of the most popular of the class of chants under notice.
> *'God rest you merry, gentlemen,*
> *Let nothing you dismay,*
> *For Jesus Christ our Saviour*

Was born upon this day,
To save us all from Satan's power,
When we were gone astray,
O tidings of comfort and joy!
For Jesus Christ our Saviour
Was born on Christmas Day.'"

Carolling parties in the streets, singing and collecting money, gradually replaced the earlier rounds made by the Waits and those made by Wassailers during Christmas's Twelve Days. The practice of singing carols around the Christmas tree, as had once been done in a circle round the Kissing Bough, is appropriate, for the word 'carol' comes to us from the Italian *carola*, meaning originally a 'ring-dance'.

However humble it is, the 'simple' carol has much to recommend it. It has a beauty and inspires a faith which is singularly suitable for this season. Almost on is own, it has redeemed what too often otherwise appears to be a Christless Christmas. It is worth noting, too, that in the relatively short time since its revival, it has had a success in crossing the boundaries of the various Christian affiliations, which has been impossible on a level of doctrinal argument.

A final preparation for Christmas is that of choosing and buying gifts for friends and family. This custom is older than Christianity itself, for the Romans had practiced a kind of charity giving during their Saturnalia. They also exchanged gifts on the *Kalends*, their New Year's Day festival. These latter presents, as in those brought by the First Foot, came to represent the giver's wishes for the recipient's health and fortune in the New Year. Such pagan associations caused the early Church to disapprove of gift-giving during the Nativity season.

In spite of this, fourteenth century English records indicate the practice was well established, but known then as 'New Year's Gifts'. These were the early ancestors of today's **Christmas presents**, given and received, as they were, within the sacred Twelve Days of the festival. Then, though, the gifts were more in the form of a contractual obligation, most often between landlord and tenant. The tenant was expected to give his landlord a present on New Year's

Day, and was assured of receiving another in return. The items given were usually food, and often became traditional ones, such as a capon being expected by a landlord from his tenant. What later came to be termed 'Christmas Boxes' were customarily given to servants, while smaller and more charitable gifts went to the Boy Bishops and to those participating in the popular Christmas Mumming Pageants.

In the seventeenth century, after some encouragement from Queen Elizabeth, the presents began to be of a more personal nature, such as clothes, and occasionally were received as early as Christmas Day. It was in this century that many of the upper classes began to keep a 'Christmas Book' in which a record was made of all presents received.

Under Cromwell, the Puritans reacted against the custom of New Year's gifts, but the bulk of the populace still held on to the enjoyable tradition. It wasn't until early in the first half of the nineteenth century that the custom of New Year's gifts began to wane and, although many still practiced it, was considered a quaint relic of earlier times. The real impetus for Christmas presents as we know them today did not come about until the 1840s. Albert's Royal tree had certainly caught the public imagination. But the popular spirit and emotion of the season were probably best expressed in Dicken's *A Christmas Carol*, published in 1843, in which the emphasis is placed on the family and in ensuring that children enjoy the festival to the fullest. Even so, up until the last part of the 1800s, many of the gifts and Christmas Boxes were not exchanged until New Year's Day. Queen Victoria was still sending New Year's gifts to her soldiers as late as the Boer War.

Today, of course, the selection of presents before Christmas has become a major preoccupation, encouraged and capitalised upon by the hype from the retail trade.   The custom has become so popular that a survey not long ago concluded that only one adult in ten, and those mostly very poor or very elderly, give no gifts at all.

Unhappily, the exchange of gifts now seems, all too often, to have re-acquired the early fourteenth century taint of obligation. As with the Christmas card, a rather queer organ of social conscience has evolved which invariably dictates that even an unwanted gift received requires another, however reluctant, in return. But then, perhaps making the effort to overcome such reluctance *may* bring us a step closer to the spirit of the season. Surely, even such an attempt is better than none at all.

And let those who anticipate Christmas with the spectre of debt it so often implies revert to the old custom of giving something made with one's own hands. How much better a homemade gift, pierced with love and reflecting the Good News we are, after all, celebrating, than an expensive appliance or a gift which has a purpose quite opposite to that of the Christian message.

Fortunately, the evolution of our secular side to Christmas giving has included a happy reminder of the charity with which the Nativity should be commemorated. This is in those gifts which arrive by surprise in the night from one, unseen and wanting nothing in return, whom delighted children throughout the world know as Santa Claus.

With the greenery up, cards received and sent, carols running through our heads and, hopefully, all the presents bought, wrapped and piled under the tree, we suddenly find **Christmas Eve** upon us. For some, there is a sigh of relief at having successfully completed the weeks, or even months of preparations. For others, panic or anticlimax might better describe the sentiment felt. Now that we have reached the eve of our landmark, how can its true significance be best honoured and appreciated? *The Roman Missal* recommends a vigil, the Mass for which concentrates on the certainty of the approaching Nativity, and on its welcome implications. The Church of England's *Book of Common Prayer* similarly includes Christmas Eve in its "Tables of Vigils, Fasts and Days of Abstinence". Certainly, for virtually all Christians, there has been a conditioning since ancestral childhoods which makes the evening of the 24th as much part of the core of the lengthy Christmas observances as the day of Nativity itself. The conditioning stems, in part, from watchful vigils the faithful have kept all through those nights which preceded the more important of the year's feast days. But the festive synthesis of the eve of the day, and of the day itself, also owes much more to other religious and secular customs which have evolved through centuries of usage.

One of the oldest of these customs is that of the **Yule Log**. Although few keep it up today, it is still widely and fondly remembered. Unbeknownst to most, its origins are as old and as pagan as those of the Druidic mistletoe. In fact, the log comes to us from the Scandinavian feast of *Juul*, at which their Thor was honoured with huge bonfires on the eve of the winter solstice.

An early influx of Nordic peoples brought the custom here, and by feudal days it had become common practice to fill the hearth with as large a log as possible. It was often so huge that it had to be drawn to the house behind straining cart-horses or oxen. While on this journey, it was usual to decorate it with greenery and even christen it with cider or ale before taking it into the house.

Tradition also deemed that money was not to change hands for a Yule Log. It had to come from one's own land, be received as a gift from a friend or a neighbour or, as a last resort, be taken from someone else's property by stealth.

The log was lit on Christmas Eve from a still unburnt piece carefully preserved from the one used the previous year. Its flame became the focal point of the evening's festivities, and warmed the wassail bowl for the season's toasts. The games played around it have varied through the ages, but medieval ones almost certainly included leap frog and blind man's buff. More importantly, the Yule Log became an emblem of the spirit of fellowship shared by all the participants upon whom its light glowed. Its flame marked the cessation, even if only temporarily of feuds between neighbours, erstwhile friends and, sometimes, within the family itself. There was also a relaxation of the usual distinctions in station between man and servant, in much the same manner as master and slave had become equals in the earlier Roman Saturnalia. In northern England, it became customary for servants to be permitted ale at their meals for as long as the log burned.

A Devon variation was the **Ashen Faggot**; ash sticks bound together by withies from the same tree. Nine such hoops were used on each faggot and, as each one burned enough to snap, it was obligatory for the host to supply a fresh round of drinks. For the larger baronial hearths, as Ashen Faggot would often be as much as seven feet in length, and weigh more than most men could lift alone.

The Yule Log's flame was sometimes nursed through all Twelve Days of Christmas, but, for smaller hearths, a minimum of twelve hours constant burning was considered sufficient. Many superstitions attached themselves to this friendly log. One of these reckoned it was an evil omen if anyone with bare feet or a squint entered the hall while it was burning. The most important superstition, though, was connected with the burning itself. Misfortune in the new year was assured for any household in which the log's flame went out of its own accord. It was critical that it be extinguished deliberately, even ceremonially, and that a piece of it be saved to protect the house against fire in the coming year, and to light the one used in the following Christmas Eve observances. The continuity provided by the flame of one Yule touching another for countless successive generations was noted by Herrick in 1630,

> *Come bring with a noise,*
> *My merry, merry boys,*
> *The Christmas Log to the firing;*

While my good dame she
Bids ye all be free,
        And drink to your heart's desiring,

With the last year's brand
Light the new block, and,
        For good success in his spending,
On your psalteries play
That sweet luck may
        Come while the log is a tending.

In spite of its ancient pagan origins, the Yule Log must surely by now be considered to have been baptised and acceptable to Christian homes, even if only as a symbolic herald of the birth of spiritual light on December 25. After all, when the alternative is central heating, how much better to warm one's Christmas Eve with a real and visible flame.

The **Yule Candle** was another customary light. If it was lit on Christmas Eve, the candle was supposed to burn during dinner, and then throughout the night as well, as a kind of living vigil. If it was lit on Christmas morning, it was kept alight until bedtime. Misfortunes, and even death, were thought to follow if it were accidentally extinguished. It was usual to put it out carefully with a pair of tongs ...and never by blowing.

Often, the candle was re-lit for each of the Twelve Days' evenings. Brand, in his *Observations on Popular Antiquities*, comments on a very large and old stone candle socket, on which the figure of an *Agnus Dei* has been chiselled out, in St. John's College, Oxford. It was used to hold an enormous Yule Candle which burned ceremoniously through the twelve Christmas suppers. As with the Yule Log, the final unburnt portion of the candle was kept through the next year as a talisman.

Christmas candles are still popular, but now they usually only differ from ordinary candles in their red or green colour, rather than in size, the factor which was once much more critical in enabling them to last through ancestral vigils.

Today, the observance of the spiritual side to Christmas Eve owes much to the traditions practiced in the parish services where childhoods have been spent. Churches are festooned with greenery for the occasion. In addition to the holly and decorated Christmas tree, a crib scene more often than not has made its appearance, surrounded by the figures of Joseph, Mary, beasts of burden, shepherds, sheep and wise men.

It was a brilliant stroke on the Church's part to use a stage-set **Nativity scene** to bring the sense of the celebration to as wide an audience as possible. Emphasising the idea that the Saviour was born in a stable had an especially graphic appeal to the poor. They could recognise and identify with the humble trappings, the manger full of straw, and participants which included an ass and an ox. In England, there was a particular appeal in the figures of sheep and shepherds "watching their flocks by night" under the great star. After all, many of the communicants were shepherds themselves.

The Offering of the Magi

The conscientious way in which they tended their own flocks gave them a vivid appreciation of what it meant to be a member of Christ's. Even the most unlettered and rudest of our ancestors, born perhaps on a straw bed under a thatched roof, could wonder at the birth in a stable of a man who would be worshipped by kings and queens in their fine palaces. If nothing else, the Nativity certainly restored a sense of dignity to the poor.

Religious veneration of the crib dates back to the seventh century when, under Pope Theodore, relics which were said to be part of the original manger were taken from Bethlehem and put in the church of *Sancta Maria ad Praesepe* in Rome. But crib adoration remained only a local phenomenon until six centuries later, when Francis of Assisi began using it at Greccio in a model of the Nativity scene. His first one, in 1223, had a live ox and ass next to the manger. And it was from Greccio that Franciscan missionaries spread the custom through continental Europe.

The crib was also enjoyed in England up until Henry VIII put an end to Papist practices. Although its popularity continued to increase in every other Christian country, the Nativity scene did not make its reappearance in English churches until the nineteenth century; and then only in those of Roman Catholic persuasion. It was not until the period between the two world wars in the twentieth century that the crib and the resurrected Nativity Play were finally accepted into Anglican and Nonconformist churches. Even then, the more staunchly Puritan members protested. Their objections, however, were overruled on the grounds that they could hardly reject a scene described in their own Bible when they were already admitting the pagan Christmas tree. Like the carol, the crib, since its revival, has had a near universal success in crossing those seemingly impenetrable boundaries between Christians.

Our Christmas Eve church services are an apposite contemporary equivalent to the penances and fasting which used to mark the occasion. Christmas Day Mass was originally held at midnight on the eve, as there had been a general consensus since the fifth century that Jesus had entered the world at that hour. For the same reason, it used to be customary for many churches to **toll the Devil's Knell** on their great bell at the stroke of midnight, inferring a funeral for Satan now that Christ's reign was at hand. The custom is still kept up at Dewsbury, Yorkshire, but in a more complicated form. There, the tenor bell sounds for each year that has passed in the Christian Era, with the last toll timed to ring out exactly at midnight. It is thought to have been started there in the Middle Ages by Sir Thomas de Soothill, who presented the church with this bell on the condition that it be tolled each Christmas Eve, partly to protect the village from the Devil's clutches in the following year, but mostly to absolve himself of a murder he had committed earlier in his life. Careful planning is required of the Dewsbury bell ringers to insure the last toll sounds at midnight. For example, if the measured rings come out at one each three second, there would be twenty tolls per minute. At that pace, for around 2000 years since Christ was born, the bell would have to commence its peals not long after ten pm.

We are more accustomed today to Christmas Eve services which include the use of candles. An interesting variation on the candle service was the **Oie'l Verrey**, practiced on the Isle of Man. There, the service started at midnight, and parishioners would bring candles with them. After prayers and a hymn, the minister would go home, leaving the congregation in the charge of his clerk. The people were then free to sing long carols by candlelight. The carols were mostly in the Manx language, and often had little in their subject matter which dealt with the Nativity. In fact, many of them had been made up by the singers themselves as part of their Christmas preparations. The songs could be up to forty verses long and, sung in alternating solos or duos, last far into the night. While the singing was going on, young maidens in the congregation would throw peas at their favourite unmarried men. After the service, most would adjourn to the closest alehouse to await the sound of the cock crowing and the welcoming dawn of Christmas Day.

While the Manx *Oei'l Verrey* custom has, in the last century, adapted itself to more conventional carols and choirs, by the time it changed, the ritual of a Christmas Eve service had caught on in English Methodist and other Nonconformist churches. But these were strictly religious and contained none of the levity, or later recourse to the public house, which had accompanied those seen on the Isle of Man.

Candles in a Christmas Eve service today are lit during the final singing of carols, a practice which is thought to have originated in mid-eighteenth century Austria, where lighted candles were taken out to the stables after the service to await the simultaneous arrival of midnight and Christ.

A beautiful and solemn tradition has evolved in some churches. On Christmas Eve, the **candle service** begins with only one or two candles lit, just enough to see the decorated tree in the shadow of the nave. As each prophecy and carol is sung, a further candle is lit. Finally, by the end of the service, when the words "I am the Light of the world" are spoken, the whole church is brilliantly aglow. The congregations then light candles which they take home to enflame and brighten their own dwellings with the Good News.

Midnight was symbolic of the darkness mankind was in before the birth of Christ. The candles symbolised the Light which had entered the world on that first Christmas. The evergreens decorating the service were a reminder of the coming spring, as well as of the concept of everlasting life. The combination of the sight of the candle flame, the scent of greenery, and the sound of carols satisfies those three of the five senses which the mystic William Blake termed the most important to this age. If the service has been Eucharistic in nature, a further sense will have been dealt with. If not, taste will be amply assuaged with the Christmas dinner on the morrow.

This nourishment of our physical selves during the final preparations can be a reminder for us to sustain our spiritual parts in at least as similar a measure, so that, when we awake on the morning of His day, it will be with the blessing of a more sublime and sacred state.

For younger members of the family, there still remains one important secular preparation before retiring to bed. This is, of course, hanging up Christmas stockings by the chimney or, if that task was performed earlier, making a final scrutiny, ensuring that theses receptacles are large enough and positioned as perfectly as possible. At many homes, a glass of milk and some cookies are left in a conspicuous location near the hearth in hopes of currying even *more* favour with the saint who so plainly and regularly demonstrates he has the power to make wishes come magically true.

Santa Claus's evolution has resulted in an archetypal figure of happiness and benevolence. In fact, his composition is complex, including at least bits of the Scandinavian Woden who carried gifts on a sleigh pulled by reindeer, the Medieval English "Old Father Christmas", the German Kris Kringle, and the fourth century Nicholas, Bishop of Myra.

For children, Santa and his presents form a symbolic worldly parallel to the coming of Christ on this date with His Good News and spiritual gifts. Santa's character today probably owes as much to Dickens's *A Christmas Carol* as it does to the popular illustrator Thomas Nast. A third and major influence on the way we see him now comes from a poem written by Clement Clarke Moore for his own children in 1822. It was originally called *A Visit from St. Nicholas*, but is now more popularly known as *The Night Before Christmas*. Moore, a professor of ancient languages in New York, was so displeased by the immense success the poem achieved, after it was published in 1823 without his permission that he refused to admit his authorship of it for another fifteen years. Our concept of Santa Claus has remained virtually unaltered since he penned those lines,

> *He was dressed all in furs from his head to his foot*
> *And his clothes were all tarnished with ashes and soot.*
> *He spoke not a word, but went straight to his work,*
> *And filled all the stockings – then turned with a jerk,*
> *And laying his finger aside of his nose,*
> *And giving a nod up the chimney he rose;*
> *He sprang to his sleigh, to his team gave a whistle,*
> *And away they all flew like the down of a thistle.*

And thus, for generations of children now, reverence has been replaced with reverie. Moore's "visions of sugar-plums dance through their heads," when and if, in their excited and weary states, they are finally able to fall asleep on this Night of nights.

External preparations have been so complex and lengthy that, when the Great Day itself finally dawns, some of us awake to it with a sense of dread, rather than one of awe. Still worse, others face it stoically and unfeelingly, looking ahead to a series of ritual duties which must, however mechanically, perforce be endured. After all, even the most obtuse among us must realise that when this day's fleeting wintry sun sets, the heart of the long-anticipated celebration will be over. There certainly appear to be grounds for a gnawing sense of anticlimax. This is particularly true if we look ahead to the seemingly interminable and cheerless winter.

Fortunately, there are others who still remember that Christmas celebrates a beginning, not an ending. They will remind us, most often from the local pulpit during the Christmas service that the whole point of the exercise has been to commemorate an event which should make us rejoice at the very ephemeral nature of life, which has given rise to what some sense as gloom.

For the more religious, **Christmas Day** may begin with a midnight mass or, as with Easter, a celebration of the sacrament at dawn. But for a greater number, a later morning Eucharistic service is customary. More often than not, these will awake to the cries of children discovering and comparing the contents of their bulging stockings. Such contents, through lengthening tradition may include some fruit in the form of a superlative apple or orange, a generous assortment of nuts and candies, and a number of small wrapped gifts. Occasionally, a much larger present or two have also arrived under the auspices of St. Nick's cloak of anonymity. But usually, the opening of the bigger presents, which wait tantalisingly under the tree, is left until later. Before the change to decimal currency, the stocking also customarily included a brand new sixpence piece, promising the anticipation of a further purchase to add to Santa's hoard.

After partaking of a light breakfast and some last minute bustle in the kitchen to ensure all will be ready for the midday feast, a **Christmas Day service** may often be in order. While its tone may have altered, the spirit of this service has changed remarkably little over the years, as can be seen from Washington Irving's description of a pre-Victorian "Christmas in an Old Hall",

"While we were talking we heard the distant toll of the

228

village bell, and I was told that the squire was a little particular in having his household at church on a Christmas morning; considering it a day of pouring out thanks and rejoicing...

On reaching the church porch, we found the parson rebuking the grey-headed sexton for having used mistletoe among the greens with which the church was decorated... So tenacious was he on this point, that the poor sexton was obliged to strip down a great part of the humble trophies of his taste before the parson would consent to enter upon the service of the day.

The parson gave us a most erudite sermon on the rites and ceremonies of Christmas, and the propriety of observing it, not merely as a day of Thanksgiving, but of rejoicing, supporting the correctness of his opinion on the earliest usages of the church, and enforcing them by the authorities of Theophilus of Cesarea, St. Cyprian, St. Chrysostom, St. Augustine and a cloud more of saints and fathers, from whom he made copious quotations. I was a little at a loss to perceive the necessity of such an array of forces to maintain a point which no one present seemed inclined to dispute; but I soon found that the good man had a legion of ideal adversaries to contend with... He concluded by urging his hearers, in the most solemn and affecting manner, to stand to the traditional customs of their fathers, and feast and make merry on this joyful anniversary of the church.

I have seldom known a sermon attended apparently with such immediate effects, for on leaving the church the congregation seemed one and all possessed with the gaiety of spirit so earnestly enjoined by their pastor. The elder folks gathered in knots in the churchyard, greeting and shaking hands; and the children ran about crying 'Ule! Ule!' and repeating some uncouth rhymes, which the parson, who had joined in, informed me had been handed down from days of yore. The villagers doffed their hats to the squire as he passed, giving him the good wishes of the season with every appearance of heartfelt sincerity, and were invited by him to the hall to take something to keep out the cold of the weather; and I heard blessings uttered by several of the poor, which convinced me that, in the midst of his enjoyment, the worthy old cavalier had not forgotten the true Christmas virtue of charity."

Irving goes on to add that, afterwards, they were all entertained "with brawn and beef, and stout home-brewed." With the exception of a squire being in usual attendance, the sequence of events has remained almost unchanged, but what is considered traditional Christmas dinner *is* quite a bit different from the one which Irving describes.

Our newer feature, which is nevertheless still a matter of individual family preference and practice, is that often, between the service and the dinner, the Yule Log or the Christmas Candle is lit, and the major presents are exchanged between family members. The principal rule involved here is that all who are at hand should be in attendance during this ritual. After all, together with marriages and funerals, Christmas continues as one of the very few occasions when families make a special effort to be together. Mother alone might be excused, for a minute or two at a time, to check on the dinner's progress in the kitchen.

The **Christmas Feast** is one of the oldest of this day's numerous traditions. As in the Roman Saturnalia, it has customarily been a time when barriers were relaxed and master and servant shared the same fare and table. Even the poorest of the community would look forward to a generous meal invariably washed down with more than usual amounts of ale, cider or wine. The devout were particular celebrants, as the feast marked an end to an abstemious Advent.

The food served up has gone through a remarkable evolution over the past 800 years. In the thirteenth and fourteenth centuries, fowl and other meat were enjoyed, along with bread made from the then expensive white flour. A goose might have provided festive fare for the humble, but for the upper class medieval table, the bird was often a swan and the other meat venison. Peacock was another favourite for those who could afford it. Its feathers and skin, which had been meticulously removed in one piece prior to the roasting, would be sewn back on before the bird was brought to the table. And, if this were not sufficient decoration, at the best houses, the beak was gilded as a final touch.

Another important and traditional English Christmas dish was the

boar's head, garnished with rosemary and bay and served on a platter of gold and silver. Often it was surrounded by a garland of holly and had an orange stuck between its teeth. Except in a very few places, this dish disappeared at the time of the Commonwealth, which followed the execution of Charles I in 1649. A notable survival of the boar's head ceremony takes place at Queen's College, Oxford, where it was originally meant to act as a compensatory feast for those boys who were unable to return to their homes for the season's festivities.

Much of the change in traditional Christmas fare came about through the rising influence of the Puritans. Using Philip Stubbes's *Anatomie of Abuse* (1583) as our spokesperson for their view of the Christmas revelry and gourmandising, we find his comments display the same acerbity they did for May Day:

> "What masking and mumming? Whereby robberies, whoredom, murder and what not, is committed? What dicing and carding, what banqueting and feasting, is then used more than in all the year besides!"

A later Puritan, William Prynne, put it even more plainly in his *Histriomastix* (1632), when he asked why heathens, seeing how we celebrate Christmas, should not think that Christ had been "a glutton, and epicure, a wine-bibber, a devil. A friend of publicans and sinners?"

Similar controversy raged over mince pies and plum-pottage. The pies, dating from as early as the fourteenth century, originally had a mutton base, and were often known as Christmas pies. Plum-pottage was an ancestor to our present Christmas pudding, and its name came from the plums, raisins and currents which went into it. The Puritans opened themselves to ridicule when they claimed that a refusal to eat either of these dishes was the same as striking a blow against Roman Catholics and other idolaters. Chambers quotes one jesting rhymester on this subject,

> *The high-shoe lords or Cromwell's making*
> *Were not for dainties – roasting, baking;*
> *The chiefest food they found most good in,*
> *Was rusty bacon and bag-pudding;*
> *Plum-broth was popish, and mince-pie –*
> *O that was flat idolatry!*

But even the Puritan zeal could not smother the popularity of Christmas and its feast. With the Restoration, Christmas came back, a little cowed and slightly tarnished, but with most of its earlier traditions intact.

It was after this that the turkey began to usurp the role which swans, peacocks and even buzzards had previously played in the Christmas meal. At that time, the turkey was still a new-comer to England, as it had first been imported from Mexico in the mid-sixteenth century. The growth in the turkey's popularity was slow but sure. Modern farming techniques have brought its price within the reach of virtually every family, and it is now considered the main attraction of the Christmas dinner. The popular preponderance of the turkey serves to illustrate how short a time is required to establish tradition. Pimlott notes it was only about half a century ago that more families were still eating chicken on Christmas Day. Now, even the goose, for many centuries the poor man's standby, has all but fallen by the wayside.

After the main course - or courses - has been consumed, dessert is usually served in the form of the Christmas cake or pudding, topped with a sprig of bright red holly berries and accompanied by the usual hot sauce. This, also, is a relatively recent innovation evolving from the earlier plum-pottages and porridges. Up until the late nineteenth century, it was enjoyed nearly two weeks later in the then more popular guise of the Twelfth Cake.

Thanks to technology, we can digest our meals while we watch and listen to another modern but, by now, well-loved and established tradition. This is the **Sovereign's Christmas Day broadcast**. The first such royal message was broadcast by wireless in 1932 by King George V, while the televised broadcasts were instituted in 1956.

The children's parties and games which are enjoyed on Christmas evening had as their precursor the **Lord of Misrule**. Like the king and queen of the bean, who would rule over the Twelfth Night parties, the Lord of Misrule was a sort of Master of Ceremonies appointed in royal or noble houses. He oversaw the masquerading, mumming, dancing and **Christmas games** which went on during the Yuletide season. Where the monarch spent Christmas, the Lord of Misrule sometimes had the title Master of Merry Disports, while at Oxford he was called Master of Revels.   One was also appointed at Cambridge, where his principal function was to oversee the production of Latin plays put on by the students.

The whimsical Lord usually ruled from Hallowtide to Candlemas, but the most famous one historically, appointed at the Inns of Court in London, held sway only for the Twelve Days of Christmas, during which time he was attended to with much pomp and ceremony.

The fervent Prynne leaves us with in no doubt as to the Puritan view on this aspect of the festivities. He condemns it as

"revelling, epicurisme, wantonesse, idlenesse, dancing, drinking, stage-plaies, masques carnalle pompe and jollity ... Hence Polydore Virgil affirmes in expres tearmes that our Christmas Lords of Misrule (which custom saith he, is chiefly observed in England), together with dancing, masques, mummeries, stage-playes, and such other Christmas disorders now in use

THE LORD OF MISRULE.

with Christians, were derived from these Roman Saturnalia and Bacchanalian festivals; which (concludes he) should cause all pious Christians eternally to abominate them."

The Lord of Misrule flourished mostly in the fifteenth and sixteenth centuries. Henry VIII ceased appointing a royal one in 1520 and, with the spreading influence of the Reformation, the practice gradually died out elsewhere. But the spirit of the custom lived on in the old games which were kept up. Brand mentions them, and so does Irving, who lists the following ones in his description of Christmas at Bracebridge Hall: "hoodman blind, shoe the wild mare, hot cockies, steal the white loaf, bob-apple, and snap-dragon." For snap-dragon, raisins were put into a shallow bowl and then brandy or another spirit was poured on them and ignited. The entertainment came from the competitors trying to snatch the raisins

from the flame. This particular game always took place after dark, and all other lights in the room were extinguished to give an added dramatic effect to the flaming bowl and the expectant faces gathered around it. A West Country variation was flapdragon, which involved drinking a mug of ale or cider into which a lighted candle had been placed.

More often than not these days, the tree and the Christmas candles will be lit again on Christmas evening. In those homes where the older customs are still observed, there is a re-lighting of the candles on the Kissing Bough. Although the Wassail Bowl has long since fallen out of favour, because of the season, hot drinks are still traditional and sensible libations.

If there is a children's party, the day may end with paper hats, crackers and some of the same games which children have played from time out of mind.

For many, the end of the twenty-fifth is a time for reflection. The preparations have been so immense, and the celebration itself seemingly so fleeting, that an understandable feeling of bewilderment might descend on finding the day has come to a close. It would be well for any thus disposed to be reminded of the meaning underlying the occasion. We emphasise the social customs and external aspects today, and yet, without the central meaning, the whole production would be a charade, or worse, a farce. Without the birth and message of Christ, there could be no Christmas. And, as Whistler points out, if the majority of people who 'pretend' to celebrate Christmas are unbelievers, it is almost certain the custom would decline and disappear. Fortunately, though, the best assurance for its survival comes from the wisdom of the ancient Church fathers, who set it to coincide with the annual rebirth of the sun. It is also useful to consider that, in spite of Puritan claims, the various social, and sometimes pagan, customs which have gathered themselves around Christmas have by now been long-blessed by centuries of Christian worship. No matter how heathen our rites may once have been, all the adornment simply serves to glorify the central meaning.

December 26, once known as the "morrow of Christmas", is the **Feast Day of St. Stephen**, who was mentioned in the early chapters of Acts. He had been a Greek Jew and was one of the first seven of "honest report, full of the Holy Ghost and wisdom" chosen to assist the Apostles as deacons. Stephen was such a sincere and zealous speaker for his new religion that an angry Jewish mob stoned him to death around AD 36, after he had accused them in no uncertain terms of having murdered Christ. Saul, later St. Paul, was still busy persecuting Christians at this time. Paul attended at, and heartily approved of, the stoning of Stephen. As this saint was the very first in a long and continuing list of those who follow Christ into martyrdom, the Church fathers appropriately fixed his feast day as the one after Christ's own. Stephen was a very popular saint in England, particularly during medieval times, and there are about one hundred and twenty-five of our churches named after him.

Bird and squirrel shooting used to be traditional pastimes on St. Stephen's Day. They stemmed in part from the much more ancient custom of **Hunting the Wren** on December 26th. This practice is thought to date as far back as the Bronze Age, when the wren was considered a sacred bird. Like the newly resurrected sun after the winter solstice, the wren was believed to be reborn after being slain. In the older traditions, a real wren would be killed and its corpse paraded through the town. The custom was once so popular in some regions that St. Stephen's acquired the name Wrenning Night. It still survives, though in a modified form, on the Isle of Man, where children beg coins in a procession carrying a green garland and decorated staves. The wren itself has now disappeared from the ceremony, except for a mention in the words of a traditional song they still sing as they make their rounds.

Blooding horses and oxen was another customary duty on St. Stephen's Day. Just as people were once bled to 'help' them recover from an illness, it was thought that the blood of the livestock became too rich and hot while they were kept idle in the stables during the holiday period. Accordingly, on December 26 a small cut would be made in their jugular veins to drain off some of the 'unhealthy' plasma. Fortunately, the animals had the rest of Christmas's Twelve Days to recover before returning to the fields on or after Plough Monday. Chambers quotes Googe's *Naogeorgus* on this,

Then followeth St. Stephen's Day, whereon doth every man
His horses jaunt and course abroad, as swiftly as he can,
Until they doe extreemely sweate, and then they let them blood,
For this being done upon this day, they say doth do them good,
And keeps them from all maladies and sicknesse through the yeare,
As if that Steven any time tooke charge of horses heare.

As barbaric as the practice sounds, it was not until the nineteenth century that it began to die out.

Today, we hardly remember St. Stephen. For us, December 26 is **Boxing Day**. As Christmas has been a time for sharing among family, St. Stephen's was one for giving to a wider, less personal circle. Clothes, food and money were given to the poor on the 26th by churches and by those better off. It gradually became traditional for most people to present a gift of money to servants, employees, apprentices, delivery people and other tradespersons one had dealt with during the year.

One of the most remarkable aspects of this holiday is that no one seems to know where the name Boxing Day came from. One answer can be found from the fact that the charitable presents used to be deposited into earthenware boxes which the collectors carried from donor to donor. At one time the collections were actually taken on St. Stephen's Day, and the earthenware receptacles were known as Christmas boxes. The 'Christmas box' is still given to trades people today, but the donation, more often than not, now takes place before Christmas. In the old days, the box could not be broken open, and the spoils got at, until December 26.

Another theory has it that the day's now popular name has come down to us from a practice the church had of opening their alms boxes and distributing the contents to the parish poor on the 26th. But the more likely explanation is that Boxing Day was derived from the boxes which employees, and latterly the poor, took on their begging rounds on St. Stephen's Day. Fortunately, the spirit of Christmas was still strong enough that few who made the effort returned empty-handed. In fact, the rewards were such that an optimistic saying arose,

> *Blessed be St. Stephen*
> *There's no fasting upon his even.*

It was only in 1871 that the Bank Holiday Act permitted employees to take Boxing Day off along with Christmas. Although this provision was originally intended only for bank employees, like other bank holidays, it has become virtually universal in application.

It is probably children who are most plagued by a sense of anticlimax on December 26. Frequently, the novelty of the long-awaited presents has already worn off. And we notice an increasing number of these gifts may no longer work if their batteries have run down. There seems nothing left to anticipate, except long and boring days at school and the chill prospect of winter. Perhaps for this reason, in the days before television (and the internet), St. Stephen's finished on a different note. In the more urban locations, for children and adults alike, the 26th was a night famed for theatrical pantomimes and harlequinades, which helped to stifle the dreary expectation of the first part of the New Year.

In the country, though, where a much less sophisticated form of entertainment was required, the ancient **Mummer's Play** helped to relieve an aching mourning for the Christmas past. The play is at least 800 years old and uses characters contemporaneous to the Crusades. Whistler points out that this makes the traditional Mummer's Play at least as ancient to Shakespeare as he is to us. It was usually performed on Christmas Eve or on the evening of Boxing Day. The words vary slightly from one region to another, but they, along with the theme, are remarkably similar when we realise the play has been handed down orally from father to son for so many generations.

The characters participating have also remained much the same. Where there are variations, it is mostly in the ways their names are spelled. Through the reign of the four Georges, St. George in some places became King George. The Saracen Turkish Knight was reduced in certain regions to the Turkey Snipe. In a few locations the latter became known as the Bold Slasher or Bold Soldier, and sometimes even as the French Beau Slasher. But aside from these minor variations, the other characters and the storyline have remained fairly constant.

Old Father Christmas usually opened the play, beginning with these lines,

> *Here come I, Old Father Christmas,*
> *Christmas or not,*
> *I hope Old Father Christmas*
> *Will never be forgot.*

The next one to come in was St. George with the words,

> *Here come I, St. George, the valiant man,*
> *With naked sword and spear in hand,*
> *Who fought the dragon, and brought him to the slaughter,*
> *And for this won the king of Egypt's daughter.*

His opponent appears and rejoins,

Here come I, a Turkish Knight,
In Turkish land I learned to fight,
I'll fight St. George with courage bold,
And if his blood's hot, will make it cold.

A battle between the two ensues and St. George emerges as a crestfallen victor. He exclaims,

Ladies and gentlemen,
        You've seen what I've done,
I've cut this Turk down
        Like the evening sun;
Is there any doctor that can be found,
To cure this knight of his deadly wound?

Fortunately for the Turk, there is another actor, the doctor, who carries an enormous box or bottle of pills, and announces,

I've a little bottle in my pocket
Called hokum, skokum, alicampane;
I'll touch his eyes, nose, mouth, and chin,
And say: "Rise, dead man," and he'll fight again.

The medicine, sometimes called Oppliss Poppliss Drops, is as effective as Christ's call to Lazarus. The Turk rises and, in spite of St. George's earlier remorse, the two engage in battle again, and the Turk is slain for the second time. The doctor is still at hand, and his miraculous medicine once again revives the fallen soldier.

A Party of Mummers

Occasionally, a few other characters also entered the drama, but only to make short inconsequential speeches, which had little, if anything, to do with the main plot. At the end, though, a final figure enters, whose speech summarises, the real reason for the performance from the Mummers' point of view,

> *Ladies and gentlemen,*
> *Our story is ended,*
> *Our money-box is recommended;*
> *Five or six shillings will not do us harm,*
> *Silver or copper, or gold if you can.*

Part of the appeal of the Mummers Play lay in the fanciful costumes they wore. Often, they also blackened their faces or wore exaggerated masks representative of the characters they were playing. But the meaning underlying the drama was far more serious, and a clue to it can be found in St. George's words comparing the slain Turk to the dying evening sun. For the miraculous resuscitation preformed by the doctor had its parallel in the resurrection all men looked for in the sun after it had passed through the dark winter solstice. And, although the characters seem to date from the Crusades, the blackened faces suggest a much earlier origin in which the plot would have revolved around the death of the Corn Spirit in the seed and in its anticipated rebirth in the spring.

In spite of being outlawed by Henry VIII, the Mummers Play's continuity survived in different rural locations up until the early years of the present century. While it has been revived in a number of places, one wonders if the effort might now be more that of nostalgia rather than the half-joking, but deeply serious, celebration of the New Year's sun.

The period between Boxing Day and New Year's Eve used to be much more important when it was recognised as part of Christmas's Twelve Days, the peasant's holiday from his labours in the field. Then, there would have been nightly feasting and revelry, illuminated by the blaze from the Yule Log. With the shift to an urban industrialised society, both jobs and holidays became harder to come by, and the Twelve Days gradually fell out of favour. There has, however, been a more recent interest in an extended holiday from December 25 to January 1. But this owes less to Christmas 's traditional Twelve Days than to a desire for a vacation bridge between Christmas and New Year's, permitting growing numbers to spend the whole of the festive period on a package holiday in a warmer clime.

December 27 is the **Feast of St. John the Evangelist**. As on St. George's Day, the saying "St. John to borrow" was popularised. This was due to a farming practice of borrowing money on the 27th to pay for seed for the New Year's crops. John is thought to have been the youngest of the Apostles and the only one to have died a natural death. Towards the end of his life he was Bishop of Ephesus. He is reputed to have been in his nineties when he died about AD 100, thus bringing the Apostolic age and the first Christian century to a close together.

December 26, 27 and 28 are each examples of three different kinds of martyrdom recognised by the Church. The first, St. Stephen's, is a case of martyrdom in will and in deed. As St; John dies a natural death, he is considered to have been a martyr in will, but not in deed. The 28th, which is Holy Innocent's Day, commemorates martyrs in deed, but not in will. It honours the children put to death at Herod's order, as described in the second chapter of Matthew.

Holy Innocents' Day was popularly known as **Childermas**. It was not a very long time ago that Christmas was considered to be a festive time for adults, and no extra provisions were made, as are today, to focus any particular attention on children. But in those pre-Santa times, children were indulged on Holy Innocents' Day instead. Often the parish church bell would be rung in memory of the martyrs and, where there was a Boy Bishop, his short reign, which had begun on December 6, would come to an end.

Even up to the present century, December 28 was believed to be one of the most unlucky days of the whole year, probably because the massacre of the Innocents was universally regarded with such horror. For this reason, no new projects were to be begun on this day, and housewives would often refuse to do any scouring or scrubbing. In fact, King Edward IV postponed his coronation by a day in 1461 when it was realised that the date originally set for it fell on the unlucky Innocents' Day.

New Year's Eve, falling as it does at the very heart of the Twelve Days of Christmas, used to be associated much more with Yuletide festivities. Now, it is temporal propinquity alone which provides a link between the two occasions. For most people, the bulk of the Christmas celebration is over with the day itself. A little bit might spill over into Boxing Day, but the evening of the 31st has become a quite separate celebration.

The Church has made the last day in the year the **Feast of St. Silvester**, a fourth century Bishop of Rome. He is hardly remembered now but, indirectly, Sylvester's influence has been quite far-reaching. It was he who baptised the Emperor Constantine, and it was the latter's Council at Nicaea that resulted in doctrinal reforms which still affect most Christian services held today.

There are a number of traditional New Year's Eve customs which still survive. One of these is a **fire ceremony** at Allendale, Northumberland, complete with Guisers. The object of the fire is to burn out the evils of the old year and to bless the crops and cattle in the coming one.

The Methodist **Watch-Night** is a newer custom. It was begun in the eighteenth century, and involves a church service which sees out the old year and starts the new one off with hymns of rejoicing. It is appropriate to consecrate an ending and a beginning in this sacred manner, but one suspects that Wesley instituted the Watch-Night as a means of removing his congregation from temptations of the revelry practiced by almost everyone else.

The much older English traditions of dancing in the New Year, or of firing a fowling piece at midnight, did not really make it into the last century. Perhaps this is just as well.   Shooting a gun at the crucial minute could have unfortunate connotations. To the young, it might be construed as a means whereby the old year was put out of its misery. To the mature, it might sound more like the starter's pistol to another year in the race of life.

If fact, to celebrate the end of one year and the beginning of the next is a strange, and even anomalous, inheritance for reasons which are all too evident. After all, aside from our birthdays, New Year's Eve, more than any other in the year, confronts us with the ideas of passing time and of inevitable change. Chambers summarises the true sentiments many feel as the clock strikes midnight,

> "At such a moment, painful reflections will obtrude themselves, of time misspent and opportunities neglected, of the fleeting nature of human existence and enjoyment, and that ere many more years have elapsed, our joys and sorrows, our hopes and our forebodings, will all, along with ourselves, have become things of the past."

The continuing popularity of **New Year's Eve toasts** and parties may owe quite a bit to the melancholy side of the date. Toasts are thought to have originated with the Greeks, who drank to their gods, magistrates and each other. The reason behind the clinking of glasses in a toast is definitely pagan. The noise was believed to drive away evil spirits which the superstitious connected with alcohol. The Danes, until they became Christians, drank to Thor and Woden. Afterwards they directed their toasts to St. Olave, who had converted them. Icelandic peoples simplified the practice further by happily toasting Christ and even God Himself.

Through the various invasions of this island, England has inherited bits of all these toasting practices. The drink was different, though, for that was traditionally Lamb's Wool from the Wassail Bowl, downed to the Saxon greeting "Waes Hael". More recently, in the southern counties, it was customary to have two toasts on New Year's Eve. The first of these was at a quarter to twelve and bid the old year adieu, while the second one was timed for midnight itself and welcomed the birth of the new cycle.

The positioning of the New Year we know today is rather curious. It has been set arbitrarily on a day which has less to do with a change in the natural rhythm than many others. The Celts and Saxons both had different times for the commencement of their annual cycles. Up until the eighteenth century, our own legal year did not begin until Lady Day on March 25th, while the farmer, who measures time from one harvest to the next, is already well into his new cycle by December 31. If we look to the heavens for a sign, we would do much better to choose the birthday of the sun at the winter solstice, rather than an inauspicious date ten days afterwards. And for the true Christian, one would suspect the real beginning came on the 25th, for it makes little sense to be in a Christian era which does not commence on Christ's birthday.

In spite of the arbitrariness of the date, and of the mixed feelings experienced on New Year's Eve, it *is* a significant signpost deserving of ceremony. There can hardly be a better method of welcoming in a time of beginnings than in the company of family and friends. More importantly, in quieter moments, the 31st provides a unique opportunity for the contemplation of change and for the drawing up of an inevitable list of resolutions. If we didn't have a New Year's Eve, when else would we take time out to examine the balance sheet of our lives and characters, and convince ourselves of the brighter prospect of improvement?

When the church bells finally "ring out the old and ring in the new", the wise among us will look forward rather than backward. If plagued by misfortune, we have been given a second chance; and if already blessed, we might at least expect more of the same. And lastly, in looking forward, we can anticipate not only the coming spring, but also the perennial delights, customs and festivals which the new advance of the seasons will bring us.

SELECT BIBILIOGRAPHY

Alford, Violet.	*Introduction to English Folklore*, 1952.

Baker, Margaret.	*Folklore and Customs of Rural England*, 1974.

Baseley, Godfrey.	*A Country Compendium*, 1977.

Bell, Adrian; Birmingham, G.A.; Blunden, E.; Brown, I.; Ford, C.B.; Mottram, R.H.;	Young, G.M.	*England's Heritage*, Revised Edition, 1961.

Brand, John.	*Observations on Popular Antiquities*, 1888.

Burland, C.	*Echoes of Magic*, 1972.

Chambers, Robert, ed.	*The Book of Days*, 2 vols., 1863-4.

Chaundler, Christine.	*A Yearbook of Legends*, 1954.

__________.	*A Yearbook of Customs*, 1957.

Christian, Roy.	*The Country Life Book of Old English Customs*, 1966.

Clarke, Hockley.	*The Unfolding Year*, 1973.

Collis, John Stewart.	*The Worm Forgives the Plough*, 1973.

Copper, Bob.	*A Song for Every Season,* 1971.

Dowse, I.R.	*The Pilgrim Shrines of England*, 1963.

Duff, Gail. *Fresh All the Year*, 1976.

Ernle, Lord.	*English Farming – Past and Present*, 6th ed., 1961.

Fidler, John.	*Discovering Saints in Britain*, 1969.

Frewin, Anthony.	*The Book of Days*, 1979.

Green, Victor J.	*Festivals and Saints Days*, 1978.

Herrick, Robert.	*The Music of a Feast*, 1968.

Hole, Christina.	*English Custom and Usage*, 1941-2.

_____.	*English Traditional Customs*, 1975.

_____.	*A Dictionary of British Folk Customs*, 1976.

Hone, William.	*The Every-Day Book*, 2 vols., 1826.

_____.	*The Year Book*, 1829.

Holt, Ellen.	*The Farmer*, 1952.

Howard, Alexander.	*Endless Cavalcade*, 1964.

Howitt, Mary, ed.	*Pictorial Calendar of the Seasons*, 1854.

Inwards, R.	*Weatherlore*, 1869.

Kirkman, F.B.	*British Birds*, 1934.

MacKenzie, Kenneth D.	*The Way of the Church*, 1923.

Marriot, Paul J.	*Red Sky at Night – Shepherd's Delight!*,1981.

Pimlott, J.A.R., *The Englishman's Christmas*, 1978.

Quiller-Couch, Sir Arthur. Ed.	*The Oxford Book of English Verse*,

New Edition,   1979.
Readers' Digest. *Folklore, Myths and Legends of Britain*, 1973.
Seymour, Aubrey. *Fragrant the Fertile Earth*, 1970.
Society for Promoting Christian Knowledge. *Saints' Days*, 1941.
Swanton, John and Clegg, John. *Nature Calendar*, 1953.
The Book of Common Prayer of the Church of England.
The Holy Bible (King James Version).
The Roman Missal, 1935 edition.
Trevelyan, G.M. *History of England*, 2nd ed., revised, 1942.
Watson, Sir James Scott. *Rural Education: The Farming Year*,
1963.
Whitlock, Ralph. *A Short History of Farming*, 1965.
________. A Calendar of Country Customs. 1978.
Whistler, Laurence. *The English Festivals*, 1947.
Wightman, Ralph. *The Seasons*, 1954.
Wright, A.R. and Lones, T.E. *British Calendar Customs: England*, 3
vols.,
        1936-8.

<u>**By the same author:**</u>
Who Am I? An Exploration of Our Essential Nature – published online with Amazon as e-book and paperback, 2022
Liberation - Awareness Yoga - A User-Friendly Guide to Patanjali's Yoga Sutras – published online with Amazon as an e-book and paperback, 2026
Awake - Conscious Pilgrimage - An Evolving Soul's Progress (Draft) by A Pilgrim (aka B E Mayne) – published online with Amazon as an e-book and paperback, 2019 (with subsequent revisions)
Awakening - Letting Go of The Imaginary Being - Encountering Fred Davis (free to view on scribd.com), 2025

<u>**Co-author - Health/Awareness**</u>
Conscious Eating – An Invitation to Intuitive Nourishment, Shaun de Warren and Brian Mayne – published online with Amazon as an e-book and paperback, 2021

<u>**Biographical**</u>
Khamara – Embracing Adversity - Living in Acceptance and Gratitude– published online with Amazon as an e-book, 2026

(As organising editor and contributor)
Shaun de Warren by Those Who Knew Him, published privately in paper and also online with Amazon as an e-book and paperback, 2022

9 781798 666326